THE JESSIE AND JOHN DANZ LECTURES

THE JESSIE AND JOHN DANZ LECTURES

The Human Crisis, by Julian Huxley
Of Men and Galaxies, by Fred Hoyle
The Challenge of Science, by George Boas
Of Molecules and Men, by Francis Crick
Nothing But or Something More, by Jacquetta Hawkes
How Musical Is Man?, by John Blacking
*Abortion in a Crowded World: The Problem of Abortion with Special
        Reference to India*, by S. Chandrasekhar
World Culture and the Black Experience, by Ali A. Mazrui
Energy for Tomorrow, by Philip H. Abelson
Plato's Universe, by Gregory Vlastos
The Nature of Biography, by Robert Gittings
Darwinism and Human Affairs, by Richard D. Alexander
Arms Control and SALT II, by W. K. H. Panofsky
Promethean Ethics: Living with Death, Competition, and Triage,
        by Garrett Hardin

Promethean Ethics

Living with Death, Competition, and Triage

Garrett Hardin

University of Washington Press
Seattle and London

Library of Congress Cataloging in Publication Data

Hardin, Garrett James, 1915–
    Promethean ethics.

    (The Jessie and John Danz lectures)
    Includes bibliographical references.
    1. Ethics. 2. Death. 3. Competition (Psychology)
4. Social ethics. I. Title. II. Series: Jessie
and John Danz lectures.
BJ1012.H28   170   79–56592
ISBN 0–295–95717–4

THE JESSIE AND JOHN DANZ LECTURES

In October 1961, Mr. John Danz, a Seattle pioneer, and his wife, Jessie Danz, made a substantial gift to the University of Washington to establish a perpetual fund to provide income to be used to bring to the University of Washington each year "distinguished scholars of national and international reputation who have concerned themselves with the impact of science and philosophy on man's perception of a rational universe." The fund established by Mr. and Mrs. Danz is now known as the Jessie and John Danz Fund, and the scholars brought to the University under its provisions are known as Jessie and John Danz Lecturers or Professors.

Mr. Danz wisely left to the Board of Regents of the University of Washington the identification of the special fields in science, philosophy, and other disciplines in which lectureships may be established. His major concern and interest were that the fund would enable the University of Washington to bring to the campus some of the truly great scholars and thinkers of the world.

Mr. Danz authorized the Regents to expend a portion of the income from the fund to purchase special collections of books, documents, and other scholarly materials needed to reinforce the effectiveness of the extraordinary lectureships and professorships. The terms of the gift also provided for the publication and dissemination, when this seems appropriate, of the lectures given by the Jessie and John Danz Lecturers.

Through this book, therefore, another Jessie and John Danz Lecturer speaks to the people and scholars of the world, as he has spoken to his audiences at the University of Washington and in the Pacific Northwest community.

v

Contents

I THE PROMETHEAN APPROACH 3

II DEATH 11

III COMPETITION 35

IV TRIAGE 56

NOTES 73

PROMETHEAN ETHICS

Chapter I

The Promethean Approach

When we deal with the deepest problems of human existence we always discover there is something more to learn from the ancients. Ethics is the study of the ways to allocate scarce resources. (This definition serves equally well for economics and ecology—which indicates the essential identity of these three disciplines.) Dilemmas created by scarcity have worried decision makers from the beginning of history. So also have the problems created by plethora, since a surplus of one thing creates a scarcity of something else. Koheleth—the Preacher—son of David who was King of Jerusalem, ended the plaint recorded in *Ecclesiastes* with the words: "Of the making of many books there is no end, and much study is weariness of the flesh."

The passage of twenty-two centuries has not lessened the force of Koheleth's complaint. Today, more than one hundred new books come off the press every day in the United States, while the world-wide production of scientific papers is something like 6,000 new articles per day.* Who can keep up with such a torrent? When I was young and foolish I vowed that I would read all the

---

* Gerald Holton in 1960 (*Science* 131:1187) estimated the number of scientific and technical articles at 1,200,000 per year; I have casually assumed that two decades have doubled this number. I know of no precise, up-to-date estimate.

This is the last footnote. Hereafter, superscript numbers in the text refer to documentation and discussion in the Notes at the end of the book. The reader, unless he has a personal reason for pursuing an issue, can safely ignore the superscripts.

articles in my small field of science. Discovering that this was impossible, I tried to read all the abstracts. That, too, proved too much. Now I know that I cannot even read all the titles. Of my earlier ambition I would say, with Koheleth, "Vanity of vanities. . . ."

A major obligation of memory is to forget. If we retained a memory of all the stimuli raining in on our senses every second we would be unable to process the data fast enough to react adaptively to new challenges. To prevent an information overload our senses and our minds have been designed (by evolution) to slough off all traces of most of the stimuli. Selective censorship is risky, but no censorship at all would be fatal. *We* are the selected products of a system of censorship that survives. It is not perfect, but it works.

Scientists and scholars must ignore most of the literature they would like to read (were they given enough time and an adequate filing system). What principles guide their selection? They are not set down in print, but something is known about them. We in the scholarly community generally ignore material published in journals that are not refereed by our peers. With respect to the rest, we let the informal network of letters and gossip amongst competitors and co-workers tell us what is worth reading and what isn't. Bias and prejudice no doubt exert their baleful influence in the selective system, but what else can we do? We have to choose somehow.

One aspect of the usual methods of selection I decry is the neglect of older writers. Among scientists anything written more than half a generation earlier is usually regarded as older and neglectable. (Really ancient classics are not given so much as a thought.) This neglect arises, I think, from the Oedipus process. Shorn of its secondary and inessential sexual meaning, the Oedipus complex of Sigmund Freud can be summarized in one brief statement: *I reject my father.* "Father," of course, is sexless, and biological parenthood not essential. What is rejected is anyone who stands in a parental relationship to the maturing adolescent.

Such a rejection is in the nature of a biological imperative: the Oedipus process is the penultimate element in the development of a fully formed individual. A young child must first accept all that the parent tells him (or her) or he will not survive; but, to become a fully independent being, he must ultimately find his own answers to the problems of his life (for fallible parents, with limited experience, cannot know all the answers). The easiest way to enter the Oedipus stage is to reject parental wisdom as well as one's parents as maturity approaches. But, compulsively followed, the Oedipus process leads to new dangers. The fully formed individual, in the ultimate stage of maturation, must finally grow beyond the Oedipus process itself, seeking other means of determining the truth.

Scholarly activities are both motivated and crippled by the Oedipus process. Each generation tends to reject the insights and the orientation of the generation before it. By and large more good than bad may come out of this rejection. I do not argue the balance, but certainly some bad comes out of it. Precious insights, perhaps inadequately supported by evidence, are lost sight of and have to be rediscovered later. At the least, the scholarly Oedipus misses the rich patina that remembrance adds to the structure of knowledge; at worst, scholarly activity becomes repetitive and inefficient.

Some of the richest insights are to be found in the oldest literature, set down before thinkers were overwhelmed with facts and what purport to be facts. Greek mythology is an ever-flowing spring of new insights. Seldom explicit (by modern standards) and usually ambiguous, a myth compels us to get our own thoughts straight as we try to deduce what the makers of a myth *might* have meant. The historical problem is probably insoluble, but we should not be deterred thereby from trying to lay bare the latent meaning. If what we discover is of value it matters little whether we found it in the ancient myth or in our own psyche.

Prometheus fascinates modern man. We have been suckled by Progress, which some take to be a simple fact though it, too, is a myth. The myth of technological progress[1] rests on two dogmas:

> *The Dogma of Aladdin's Lamp*: If we can dream of it, we can invent it.
> *The Dogma of the Technological Imperative*: When we invent it, we are required to use it.[2]

Because he stole fire from the gods and gave it to man, the Titan Prometheus is often held up as the archetypical technologist, the father of "progress" before the word was coined. If that is the whole meaning of Prometheus then we can say that a fine presentation of the Promethean spirit is to be found in the writings of the physicist Freeman Dyson. I will briefly present his argument, and then point out why I think it is seriously wrong.

While admitting that pesticides and drugs should be subject to some societal control because of the harm they may do, Dyson argues that the hidden costs of saying "No" to technology require that we sometimes support otherwise dubious developments in order to keep up the morale of scientists and engineers.[3] Specifically, he acknowledges that an American SST (supersonic transport plane) would have been an economic failure but says that we should have gone ahead with it anyway in order to keep up the spirits of the engineers who designed it, so that they could think up even more extreme innovations in the future. A curious argument, made even more curious by Dyson's supporting it with a quotation from William Blake, whose unforgettable line about England's "dark, Satanic mills" can hardly be interpreted as a glorification of technology. Nevertheless, Dyson triumphantly quotes Blake as a justification of every new technology: "You never know what is enough unless you know what is more than enough." In other words, *Experiment now—Repent later.* Such is the Dogma of the Technological Imperative, which Dyson embraces.

Prometheus was wiser. When Zeus learned of the gift of fire to mankind he became indignant: he summoned other gods to set a trap for the Titan. They formed a woman out of clay; one god gave her life and dressed her, another gave her jewelry, and another flowers. Aphrodite gave her beauty and charm while Hermes taught her guile and treachery. Her name was Pandora—"All Gifts." The gods also gave her a jar filled with evils and diseases, confident that her curiosity would impel her to open it. No doubt she herself was intended to be a gift to Prometheus; but, if so, she was rejected by him, and then accepted by his brother, Epimetheus.[4]

From the accounts that have come down to us it is not completely clear that Prometheus was given a chance to reject Pandora. The best evidence for this interpretation lies in the names of the two brothers: Prometheus means *fore-thinker*; Epimetheus, *after-thinker*. Prometheus, offered the beautiful gift, must have said something like this to himself: "What a beauty! What pleasure I can have in her—today. *And then what?* What happens tomorrow, and next year? Why are the gods offering me this?"

And then what?—this is the ecologist's question, the question of the fore-thinker, Prometheus' question. Epimetheus was no ecologist: he took the short-term gain, together with its consequences, which, perforce, he thought about afterwards.

The total Promethean is both technologist and fore-thinker. Dyson, and most of our technologists, should be called Epimetheans. The Sorcerer's Apprentice was also an Epimethean: he did not ask "And then what?"

Whatever Blake may have meant by his statement, his words can be given a defensible interpretation. "You never know what is enough unless you know what is more than enough," said the poet: the question is, *know* by what means? If the knowing is by direct, personal experience the advice is not defensible. A person who wants to learn what is more than enough when it comes to jumping off high buildings might jump off higher and higher ones until he finds out. But Nature selects against such Epimethean behavior.

A Promethean seeks knowledge in other ways: he uses expendable substitute species and develops general theories of motion, acceleration, and force to enable him to predict what is more than enough without personally experiencing it. Theory is vicarious experience. To insure that we do not overlook any good opportunities it is advisable that we *know vicariously* what is more than enough. We have no reason to think that that is what Dyson meant. To know danger vicariously and to take forethought to avoid it, is to become a true Promethean.

After two centuries of Progress-intoxicated Epimethean behavior the United States took a great Promethean step in January of 1971 when NEPA—the National Environmental Protection Act—was signed into law. NEPA requires a Promethean analysis of every proposed intervention in the environment before it can be carried out. As the world becomes more and more crowded with human beings it is harder to do anything to the environment without harming somebody, somewhere. The greater the crowding, the greater the harm, and the more probable the harm. The Epimethean assumption, "Innocent until proven guilty," was tolerable in earlier, uncrowded days; from now on, only the Promethean assumption, "Guilty until proven innocent," is a safe guide to action.[5]

To become fully Promethean we must learn to question the unquestionable. This is, to put the matter mildly, not easy. "Unquestionable" implies psychological repression, which is always easier to see in others than in ourselves. We must, so to speak, lift ourselves by our bootstraps; we must uncover our own taboos.

In the remainder of this book I shall deal with three topics that are more or less afflicted with taboo: death, competition, and triage. I think it is true that most people reject—or repress the thought of—one, two, or all three of these entities. Their opposites, however—life, cooperation, and compassion—are accepted as unquestioned goods. Goods they are indeed, but I insist that we must take seriously the question raised by Cervantes' curate: *"But can we have too much of a good thing?"*[6] I insist that this is not a rhetorical question, and that the answer to it is *Yes*. So also argues the English barrister John Sparrow in his wise little book, *Too Much of a Good Thing.*[7] Environmentalists know that a little phosphate poured into a lake increases algal growth and the crop of fish, but too much causes such an overgrowth that the lake "dies," becoming useless for human beings. A little carbon dioxide released into the air increases plant growth; too much may turn the world into a greenhouse, heating it up to a level at which the polar ice caps melt, submerging most of the major cities of the world. A little crowding of human beings produces the complex and ill-understood conditions needed for that undefined good we call "civilization"; too much crowding produces irritation and anarchy.

So also can there be too much life, too much cooperation (too little competition, really), and even too much compassion, as that term is ordinarily understood. (Properly understood, I think there cannot be too much compassion, but that is because "properly understood" is undefined.) The task of Prometheus—our task—is vicariously to know ahead of time what is too much of each good thing so that we do not make the mistake of striving for the bad of too much good.

What I present here is a sketch of the principles of Promethean ethics, the ethics that is obsessed with time. One might suppose that ethical discussions have always devoted much attention to time, but this is not so. Our possible obligations to posterity cannot be discussed without considering the effect of the passage of time on values. Ernest Partridge reports the almost complete lack of discussions of the posterity issue in philosophical journals.[8] A search through all ten annual issues of *The Philosopher's Index* (which lists papers printed in some two hundred philosophy journals) uncovered only about a dozen papers on posterity. A computer scan of the titles of nearly 600,000 Ph.D. theses carried out in 1978 turned up *zero* titles with the phrase "unborn generations" in them, *zero* with "future generations," and only one with "posterity"—Partridge's own dissertation, *Rawls and the Duty to Posterity*.

Of course, titles do not cover all the topics treated in dissertations, but in a population of 600,000 theses-titles one could reasonably expect a larger representation of posterity-oriented titles if in fact a concern for posterity were a burning issue in contemporary philosophy. Perhaps we dare hope for more in the future because of the growing concern with the environment. Perhaps the founding of the journal *Environmental Ethics* in 1979 is a straw in the wind.

Most systems of ethics are overwhelmingly personalistic and present-oriented. Buber's *I and Thou*[9] can be fairly categorized as an *I-Thou, Here and Now* approach.[10] A similar criticism cannot be leveled against Fletcher's *Situation Ethics*,[11] which is splendidly ecological in its outlook. If the approach I present here is at all different from Fletcher's it is only in the *emphasis* placed on time-bound processes. Whenever we are faced with a recalcitrant moral question I hold that it is essential to ask, "What is the Promethean answer?" What happens when we challenge each postulated good with the question *And then what?* The way Promethean ethics[12] works will be illustrated with only three particular topics, but the principles are quite general and can be—in fact, should be—extended to other areas.

Chapter II

Death

Death has suddenly become a live topic: a generation ago it was pretty much under a taboo. Jessica Mitford castigated Americans for treating death as an obscenity.[1] So successful was her book, *The American Way of Death*, that it brought about its own obsolescence. Instruction in the art of dealing with the dying patient is now an integral part of the curriculum of theological seminaries. Physicians, though psychologically threatened by the dying patient whom they see as an adverse judgment on their professional competence, are now trying to accept death as a natural event. There is even a journal called *Thanatology*. That so great a change in public attitude took place in one short generation justifies, to my mind, much optimism about the possibility of other reforms in the future. Taboos can be dissolved. Stupidities can be avoided. People can change.

The problem of dying with dignity is a personal problem that requires personalized help: there is not much an impersonal book can do about it. But the prestige of science has endowed our society with a remarkable amount of objectivity: people, despite their self-centeredness, do want to know the reason for things. Conventionally we contrast emotion and objectivity, but the healthy, objective person experiences an emotional satisfaction in knowing the objective reasons for things. In *Paradise Lost*, Milton promised he would "justify the ways of God to men."[2] Those of us who no longer admit to a belief in God still welcome a justification of Nature's ways, particularly when we face a prospect that does not fulfill the heart's desire.

Why is there such an event as death? A superficial acquaintance with natural science may lead one to regard death as a sort of accident, a defeat, a pathological event. The theory of evolution, which Spencer summarized in terms of "survival of the fittest," is wrongly interpreted to mean that there is an irrepressible "instinct for self-preservation" which takes precedence over all other impulses. A plausible hypothesis, but subtly and gravely wrong, as a curious example from nature shows.[3] Richard Alexander tells of a particular species of cricket in which the mother allows herself to be eaten alive by her own children, thus giving her offspring a better start in life and increasing the probability of their surviving. The cricket mother certainly obeys no instinct for *self* preservation: the preservation of her "germ line" takes precedence. Evidently, given the total pattern of life of this particular species, the germ line is better preserved by personally-selfless–progeny-altruistic behavior than it would by personally-selfish–progeny-neglecting behavior. We *know* this is the correct explanation, for the mutation process (which is unstoppable) would sooner or later produce a personally selfish mother who (if such behavior actually increased the probability of having grandchildren) would replace the present natural type. The explanation just given is the sort often used in what is now called "sociobiology" (which is new more in name than in fact): in brief, gene-preservation takes precedence over self-preservation.[4] All arguments for this conclusion reduce to one final rhetorical question: *How could it be otherwise?* This question is unanswerable and decisive.

It may be objected that the cricket story is quite exceptional, that this is the story of only one species among millions. True, but the moral of the exceptional tale is perfectly general. In many species, certainly among all mammals, parents sacrifice *something* of themselves to further the interests of their children. Complete egoism on the part of the parents simply does not pay, not in an evolutionary sense. The shortening of a parent's life is a trivial matter if the probability of there being children—and grandchildren and more remote descendants—is increased by the sacrifice. In a word, and almost paradoxically, death has survival value. In a strict and narrow biological sense, the death of the individual is *good* if it benefits the germ line. So the paradox is only apparent.

Lest it be supposed that only altruism is selected for within the family circle, let me cite another variation in behavior. The European Swift lays a clutch of three eggs in the early summer, the offspring of which must be fed by the parents later, gleaning insects on the wing. Not many insects fly in cold, rainy weather. If the weather turns unfavorable while the eggs are being brooded the parents tip first one egg out of the nest, then two, and finally all three.[5] The parents' action is the avian equivalent of abortion. The adaptive significance is obvious: parents who carry out such "abortion" will, on the average, leave more living offspring behind than will parents who unwisely—that is, unseasonably— bring young into the world at a time when they cannot take care of them.

Applying conventional human language to these two animal stories we would likely speak of the noble self-sacrifice of the cricket mother, and the despicable murderousness of the swifts. *Bio*-ethically, however, the two cases are identical: each strategy maximizes survival *in the long run*. Both species are, so to speak, accurate Promethean calculators: their instinctive behavior takes account of the *And then what?* question. As a matter of fact, *all* species are Promethean calculators—except possibly Homo sapiens, some of the members of which suffer from the romantic delusion that we can survive as Epimetheans.

Paradoxically, shortness of life can have survival value. How length of life is determined by evolutionary forces has been convincingly explained by R. A. Fisher[6] and Peter Medawar.[7] Human efforts to escape the effects of natural selection[8] often take the form of *commonizing*[9] the rewards, a dangerously Epimethean strategy found in such inventions as social security systems, socialized medicine, and "progressive" taxation. These topics deserve, and will no doubt some day receive, a thorough study from the Promethean point of view. For the present let us pass them by.

The value of death is influenced by the formative stage of the individual at the time when life is terminated. We can distinguish three major states:

> the newly forming,
> the malformed,
> the dysforming.

The newly forming are individuals in the various early stages of development—by name, zygotes, embryos, and fetuses. These stages have not the form of adults, nor can they function like adults. Though poor in form they are rich in information, the information needed to produce the adult form—given about twenty years of expensive investment of love and effort. The objective value of an embryo is very little because little has so far been invested in it; the embryo is a large lien on the future, should it be saved. When the principal investor of love, time, and effort—the pregnant woman—feels she cannot afford a further investment there is no rational reason for the community to impose this lien on her future. The community will lose, not gain, if it denies an abortion to a woman who asks for it; if, to put the matter another way, the community adopts a policy of mandatory motherhood.

This should be obvious, but it isn't. We are the inheritors of some otherwise valuable traditions that interfere with rationality. To understand them let us go back to a United Nations conference convened in Bucharest in August of 1974. Among the nongovernmental organizations (NGOs) submitting statements was one that called itself the "Pro-Life Bucharest Team." The heart of the statement by this NGO follows:

> . . . we wish to assert that the value of each human individual is absolute. In other words, every human life has to be valued absolutely, precisely because it is a human life—not depending merely on its social value, state of development, likelihood of enjoying health, wealth, longevity or well-being in general.
>
> We utterly reject all concepts of "unwanted people" or "Lives not worth living" or "Too many people," as being a denial of human rights and pointing in a totalitarian direction.
>
> We apply this specifically to the unborn, the incurably sick, the abnormal and the old.
>
> We utterly reject the practices of abortion, euthanasia, infanticide, and unnatural methods of fertility control.

As one who holds opposing opinions I object first to any group arrogating to itself the term "pro-life," implying that those who differ with them are against life. I know no one who is truly against life. The real issue is whether life is uniquely a thing of which there cannot be too much. The Bucharest group implicitly denies the "too much" principle, opposing even "unnatural methods of birth control." Their statement shows a fine consistency. In contraception, spermatozoa (100 million of them per day), eggs (one per month), or both, have the life taken from them. It is not surprising that Pro-Lifers who have learned a little bit of biology should be opposed to contraception.

The ideal of preserving all life can have little influence on what happens to the gametes. The normal functioning of a healthy young male condemns 100 million spermatozoa to death every day regardless of his behavior. If contraception doesn't kill his gametes, nocturnal emission or normal resorption by the gonads will. For male gametes, death is the norm, continued life the rare exception. The situation is less extreme in the female sex. Releasing one egg per month (out of an initial store of perhaps 30,000) a woman produces about 400 fertilizable eggs in her lifetime. It is a rare woman who has twenty children, though such monstrous fertility would still entail the early death of 95 percent of her eggs. In a healthy society living under conditions of zero population growth (ZPG), the average woman produces only a bit more than two children, which means that more than 99 percent of her eggs lose their life early. Once we understand the necessity of the natural wholesale death and dissolution of the earliest stages of life we cease to react emotionally to the death of a few more gametes (or fertilized eggs, for that matter). Our ethical ideas cannot help but be influenced by numbers.

To their credit it should be said that most Pro-Lifers, or Right-to-Lifers (the common term in America), do not take so extreme a stand as the Bucharest group. Those who are Catholic are *supposed* to oppose contraception, but in fact most American Catholics do not, their reproductive behavior differing only slightly from that of American Protestants. The fact that most American Right-to-Lifers do not oppose contraception—the killing of living human gametes—shows that, at least to this extent, they recognize the wisdom of the "too much" principle.

Why must we say that there can be "too much of a good thing"? Basically, it is because we recognize that no thing, good or bad, exists in a vacuum. It is surrounded by other things, good and bad. The whole is bound into an elaborate and only partially understood network of relations, the elements being so tied together that "we can never do merely one thing."[10] Most importantly, we can never maximize more than one variable at a time,[11] and when we insist on maximizing one variable we can be quite sure that we are driving many others toward their respective minima. With the support of modern medicine we might be able to maximize the number of children at around twenty per woman, but this maximization of the quantity of life would surely soon minimize the quality. (The fact that it is difficult to give a clear and unique definition of the "quality of life" is not adequate ground for discarding the concept.)

The recognition of the essential conflict between the quantity and the quality of life is very ancient, as we see by consulting *Ecclesiastes* once more:

> To everything there is a season,
> And a time to every purpose under the heaven:
> A time to be born, and a time to die;
> A time to plant, and a time to pluck that which is planted;
> A time to kill, and a time to heal . . .[12]

This is the ecological view, the time-bound Promethean wisdom. What a world of suffering is caused by Epimethean one-variable maximizers! Time matters. The season matters—the season of life. Death has different meanings, different significations at different periods of life.

Let us continue to focus on the problem of death in the earliest stages. These are the stages before birth, and the individual at this time should never be referred to as an "unborn child," for that would deny the reality of the easily observable differences between embryos and born children. (The propagandistic reason for denying the distinction is obvious, of course: Right-to-Lifers want to conceptually graft into the embryo abilities, perceptions, and legal rights only found in, or appropriate to, the stages after birth.) The earliest stages of Homo sapiens, like the earliest stages of all multicellular animals are more potentiality than realization. An embryo is like the replaceable blueprint for a great building:

it is a nearly valueless set of information for a structure that will be valuable in the future, after a great deal more is invested in the realization of its potential.[13]

I will not spend time here on a detailed justification of freedom of choice in abortion, because I have (I think) already dealt adequately with this topic in my book *Mandatory Motherhood*.[14] However, before going on to other topics let me present a brief historical survey of abortion in western civilization.

Abortion opponents commonly suppose (and sometimes say) that abortion has been almost universally disapproved of since time immemorial, and that it is only in the decadent present that anyone pretending to a moral conscience has seriously defended the practice. This is quite untrue, as the studies of Himes[15] and Devereaux[16] amply show. Almost everywhere, and at almost all times, abortion has been approved of by the sex capable of employing it, though in many societies the sex which enjoys the natural luxury of never having abortions, often disapproves of the practice. Focusing only on the European civilization we see that it was long divided into two subcultures, male and female. Until recently these have been distinguished in this way:

> The male subculture has been literate and theoretical, the female subculture nonliterate and practical. The written analysis of sexual problems has been carried out by males who certainly never had the experience of having children; many of them [e.g., celibate clergy] did not even have the experience of living and sharing with the child-bearing subculture. With such a separation of experience and theory-construction it is scarcely to be wondered at if male theories often bore little relationship to reality. Those who are trained in the sciences know how essential it is to keep theorizers close to the growing edge of experience. It is hard for scientists to take seriously the vast bulk of theological writings on motherhood. Women have children, and men write books on theology.[17]

This account is in agreement with James Mohr's,[18] from which it appears that the history of abortion in America can be divided into these periods:

1. Until 1820: the traditional two subculture period, with abor-

tion freely practiced. (Freely, though perhaps not commonly, under frontier conditions.)

2. From 1820 to 1870: the merging of the two subcultures, resulting in the passage of abortion-prohibition laws by the male subculture, the only group then allowed to sit in legislatures.

3. From 1870 to 1958: a fairly stabilized system of prohibition and hypocrisy, with illegal abortions rising to around a million per year. The liquidation of hypocrisy began with the publication of *Abortion in the United States*.[19]

4. From 1958 to 1973: the abortion reform movement, ending in the *Roe* v. *Wade* decision of the Supreme Court, which established freedom of choice for abortions in the first trimester of pregnancy, with limited (and vague) restrictions in the second.

After 1973, what? At first it seemed as though women would have the freedom they had enjoyed before the two subcultures began merging, but the rapid rise of Right-to-Life pressure groups cast doubt on this optimistic prognostication. The future is unclear. It is not easy to disrupt the cultural patterns created by more than a century of repression, during which time (1820–1958) the cultural memory of thousands of years was pretty nearly erased. F. A. von Hayek has stated the conservative view of cultural change in its most extreme form: "The brain is an organ enabling us to absorb, but not to design culture."[20] This cannot be completely true because cultures *do* change in time, but Hayek's statement reminds us how limited the power of pure rationality is in bringing about cultural change in the face of strong emotional resistance. Time—the succession of generations—is required. The period of fifteen years from 1958 to 1973—only half a generation —was perhaps too short a time to bring about a stable reversion to the time-tested morality of our *foremothers*. (That publicists have recently felt obliged to coin this word, the correct term in the present context, is but one more evidence of the reality of the two subcultures.)

What about death among the second of the three classes distinguished earlier, namely among the malformed? This class is by far the least numerous, but the problems it raises are much the most difficult—morally, psychologically, and legally. Acting without consensus, medical personnel continue to eliminate some of the malformed, principally by "benign neglect";[21] there is a small philosophical literature on the subject.[22] I do not at present feel competent to treat the ethics adequately, and so will pass on to the last and most numerous group of all, the group to which all of us some day will belong, if we live long enough.

I call this group the class of "the dysforming." The word is a newly coined one, using the prefix *dys-* which carries the flavor of bad, hard, or unlucky, a prefix already familiar to us in the words "dyspepsia," "dyslexia," and "dysfunction." Old age is the dysforming age. The normal form then becomes distorted by tumorous growths (benign and malignant) and by shrinkages of the long bones and cartilages, resulting in diminished stature. Even the behavior of the senile is, at bottom, caused by dysforming processes in the brain, where neurons wither away and synapses disconnect. The aged are subject to degradative processes that can be expected to go on so long as life lasts. In the "newly forming" stage of our existence we can expect to achieve a normal form with further development; the malformed can sometimes be *re*formed by the surgeon's art; but for the dysforming nervous system there is no hope of effective reformation. Death is the only plausible corrective of dysformation.

Scientists, being no more than human, sometimes are as foolish as other people in their wishful thinking, even in areas where they should know better. A most brilliant twentieth-century scientist, J. D. Bernal, at the age of sixty-six wrote: "Death has been and always remains a personal and social tragedy, but inevitable and necessary as it has been in the early history of organic evolution, it is abundantly clear that it no longer fulfills a useful role in human societies."[23] Bernal is wrong on several counts: only rarely is death a social tragedy; death need not be a personal tragedy; and it is abundantly clear that death will always fulfill an important, even essential, role in human society. In fact, it is hard to escape concluding that the social importance of death will become even greater in the foreseeable future.

Science is cumulative wisdom. What a pity it is that the accumulation that most scientists draw upon is restricted to the official literature of science. Much scientific wisdom can be found outside the mainstream of science, in poetry, novels, and histories. Jonathan Swift (1667–1745) showed a profound understanding of the nature of death in *Gulliver's Travels*, written more than two centuries before Bernal. In the third voyage, Gulliver encounters a kingdom where a tiny minority, called the *Struldbruggs*, "enjoy" immortality.[24] Upon being informed of these people Gulliver exclaims, "I cryed out as in a Rapture: Happy Nation, where every Child hath at least a Chance for being immortal! . . . Happiest beyond all Comparison are those excellent *Struldbruggs*, who being born exempt from that universal Calamity of human Nature, have their Minds free and disengaged, without the Weight and Depression of Spirits caused by the continual Apprehension of Death." The normal natives soon disillusion Gulliver, who learns that:

> When they [the Struldbruggs] came to Fourscore Years, which is reckoned the Extremity of living [for the normal majority] in this Country, they had not only all the Follies and Infirmities of other old Men, but many more which arose from the dreadful Prospect of never dying. They are not only opinionative, peevish, covetous, morose, vain, talkative; but uncapable of Friendship, and dead to all natural Affection, which never descended below their Grandchildren. Envy and impotent Desires, are their prevailing Passions. But those Objects against which their Envy seems principally directed, are the vices of the younger Sort, and the Deaths of the old. By reflecting on the former, they find themselves cut off from all Possibility of Pleasure; and whenever they see a Funeral, they lament and repine that others are gone to an Harbour of Rest, to which they themselves never can hope to arrive.

In considerable detail Swift accurately describes the state that characterizes all old people sooner or later, namely (in the words of a contemporary) "the loss of all interests outside themselves."[25] This decay into pure egotism is an understandable consequence of the increasing loss of contact between the ego and the outside world. The senses become less keen. Memory fails. Swift had the acuteness to notice that it is the memory of recent events that fails faster than memory for the events of childhood. (Nature has here a sure recipe for producing a social bore.) Swift also notes that what psychologists now call short-term memory—the rapidly decaying memory of the last few seconds—fails in the old. For this reason, says Swift, "they never can amuse themselves with reading, because their Memory will not serve to carry them from the Beginning of a Sentence to the End." The failure of short-term memory is responsible for much that annoys us in the senile.

Obviously those who dream of doing away with death, dream also of putting a stop to the aging process. But there is another aspect to living a long time that falls outside the physiological process of aging and dying:

> Language . . . being always upon the Flux, the *Struldbruggs* of one Age do not understand those of another; neither are they able after two Hundred Years to hold any Conversation (farther than by a few general Words) with their Neighbours the mortals; and thus they lye under the Disadvantage of living like Foreigners in their own country.

One can plausibly argue that even without physiological deterioration the psychological evolution of the individual would carry him past a "point of no return," making rapport with young people more difficult and finally impossible. It is hard to imagine a ninety-year-old, no matter how healthy or well-preserved, teaching in a nursery school. How much fun would a 640-year-old Chaucer have in a contemporary discotheque?

If this argument is sound, even the conquest of physiological aging would not make immortality a blessing for the individual. One must conclude that Bernal, though a good scientist, was not a good science-fictionist. Swift was. Science-fiction serves the Promethean purpose of furnishing us with cost-free "thought experiments" whereby we may examine the goals of scientific research before we subsidize the means.

A striking feature of the literature on death is the frequency with which one first-class thinker contradicts another. Two philosophers from the seventeenth century serve to illustrate the point.

"There is nothing more real than death, nor more terrible," said Pascal. Retorted Spinoza: "A free man thinks of nothing less than of death; and his wisdom is a meditation not of death, but of life."

Like most people of my time and place I agree with Spinoza. I am astonished that Pascal should say that death is the most real of things. Death is a kind of zero. Is zero real? The concept of zero as a place-holder in the numerical system is immensely useful, but there is no real *thing* called zero. "Division by zero is forbidden," says the algebraist, and for good reason. It is one of the wonders of history that Pascal, so good a mathematician, could have spawned so much nonsense in philosophy.

Nonsense is seductive. In our own day the Spanish philosopher Miguel de Unamuno has given a passionate defense of Pascal's position:

> The tragic Portuguese Jew of Amsterdam wrote that the free man thinks of nothing less than of death; but this free man is a dead man, free from the impulse of life, for want of love, the slave of his liberty. This thought that I must die and the enigma of what will come after death is the very palpitation of my consciousness. When I contemplate the green serenity of the fields or look into the depths of clear eyes through which shines a fellow-soul, my consciousness dilates, I feel the diastole of the soul and am bathed in the flood of the life that flows about me, and I believe in my future; but instantly the voice of mystery whispers to me, "thou shalt cease to be!" the angel of Death touches me with his wing, and the systole of the soul floods the depths of my spirit with the blood of divinity.
>
> Like Pascal, I do not understand those who assert that they care not a farthing for these things, and this indifference "in a matter that touches themselves, their eternity, their all, exasperates me rather than moves me to compassion, astonishes and shocks me," and he who feels thus "is for me," as for Pascal, whose are the words just quoted, "a monster."[26]

"I feel the diastole of the soul"—what lovely words! But are such feelings *evidence* of immortality? And can we decisively refute our opponent by calling him "a monster"? Many of the questions treated in philosophy and theology are outside the realm of evidence, as that term is ordinarily understood. We can understand (though we need not condone) the deep believers who resort to elevated rhetoric or descend to opprobrium to shore up a position that is not, and so far as we can see cannot be, *operationally* supported.[27] Some people feel they have an immortal soul and some do not: let's leave it at that. I confess I belong in the latter category.

How, then, can we explain the enduring impulse to postulate an unobservable soul and an unprovable life after death? (Those of the opposite persuasion will ask how can anyone *not* believe in a death-defying soul? But I will not present their case because I cannot fairly do so.)

"It is significant," says the Reverend Samuel Brandon, "that in few religions has death been regarded as a natural event."[28] Why should *human* death not be natural? Several conjectures are plausible. From a personal point of view, death is certainly the rarest of events. Egoistically (at least until religion gets its licks in) death seems undeserved, and it is only a step from "undeserved" to "uncaused," or nonnatural. But if the cause is nonnatural, what is it? Demonic powers are almost universally blamed. The Christian religion has been somewhat exceptional in its emphasis on divine (as opposed to demonic) causation. But it was the Christian hypothesis that made Milton feel he had "to justify the ways of God to men," for, if God is good, how can He tolerate a "bad" like death? If God is flawless it must be men who are flawed, and Paul put his finger on the essential point: "The wages of sin is death."

Paul's statement takes on new meaning as it is worked over by the unconscious. *At the unconscious level* rhetorical qualifications do not exist: the Pauline predication becomes "The wages of sin is *always* death." Also at the unconscious level the mind falls into what logicians call the Fallacy of Affirming the Consequent—in this case, interchanging the principal elements and asserting that death is always the result of sin. Mortals being less than saintly it is easy, *ex post facto*, to explain every death by some conveniently remembered antecedent sin.

The religious explanation of death seems particularly tortured, however, when an infant dies before it has had a decent chance to be sinful. In the days when infant mortality was high the death of

innocent infants was a painful puzzle. The Judeo-Christian tradi-
tion had an answer of course: original sin, the sin of Adam and
Eve of which each mortal inherits his or her share. By the postulate of original sin, religion created a waterproof system—which
explains nothing because it explains everything. Belief in original
sin encouraged the horror of death. Death casts aspersions on
one's virtue: how can the ego tolerate such a judgment?

There is another root to belief in immortality. In Greek mythology Thanatos (Death) is the twin brother of Hypnos (Sleep).
Psychologically this makes sense for both cause consciousness to
evaporate. The consciousness evaporated by Hypnos soon re-
turns; Ego has no doubt that the same person exists before and
after the puzzling hiatus. Then (some ask), is it not reasonable
to suppose that the Ego-made-unconscious by Thanatos will also
regain consciousness later, either in a resurrection of the original
Ego (as in Christian eschatology) or in the personality of another
human being or even another animal (as in the reincarnation of
Eastern religions)? Quite plausible; quite unprovable; quite undis-
provable. What more can be said?

In trying to find reasons for ancient beliefs we generally lean
heavily upon the unconscious, on egoistic greed, and on irratio-
nality. But should we not also at least explore the possibility that
rationality and the disinterested striving for knowledge play a
role? Assuming that which I cannot prove, let me present a plausible argument.

A most fundamental idea of rationality is the *conservation assumption*, the idea that things are neither destroyed nor created,
merely changed in some way. Double-entry bookkeeping rests
on this idea, as does the economic axiom, "There's no such thing
as a free lunch." In the nineteenth century, science made explicit
the ideas of the conservation of matter and energy, but surely a
dim appreciation of these ideas pervaded science from the earliest
days. In the light of our impulse to conserve, the invention of the
soul is understandable. When a person dies there is no obvious
change in mass or weight. A subtle change can be postulated. The
word "spirit" originally meant breath, but came to mean soul:
the breath can be weighed (though, with antique apparatus, not

easily). People might have tried to capture the soul by saving the dying breath (expiration) but there is no evidence that any experimenter did so. Probably early scientists had a gut feeling that what was lost in death was something outside the laws of conservation.

If so, they were right. Death, which is certainly not a *thing*, is the mere absence of life—which also is not a *thing*. We invoke the word life to stand for an undefined complex of functions that exists because of the organization of the parts, or the information encoded in the organized parts. Matter and energy obey conservation laws; information and organization do not. When information or organization are destroyed *they are destroyed utterly*, without residue (other than the non-thing we call chaos). Thoroughly shuffle a newly purchased deck of cards and nothing of the original organization remains. Smash a watch with a hammer and only the matter and energy of the original object is conserved. Crush a living cell (the fantastic complexity of whose organization we still do not understand) and all its "life" vanishes without a trace. Disappearance is always puzzling to the enquiring mind, but nothing is gained intellectually by giving a name to a presumably conserved entity (soul) when confronted with the disappearance of information, for information is not subject to conservation laws.

This wisdom, like most true wisdom, is very old. Also, like most fundamental ideas, some of its earliest presentations were nominally humorous. In a fragment of the writings of Epicharmus, a Sicilian comic poet of the fourth century B.C., one of the characters says, "I am not afraid of being dead; I just do not want to die." Spoken on the stage in a burlesque of cowardice one can imagine the guffaws this joke elicited. But, as Freud said, no joke is merely a joke.

A bit more than a century later Epicurus (344–270 B.C.) returned to the idea of the nothingness of death and wrote what is still the last word on death, operationally viewed:

> Death, the most terrifying of ills, is nothing to us, since so long as we exist death is not with us; but when death comes, then we

do not exist. It does not concern either the living or the dead, since for the former it is not, and the latter are no more.[29]

The living, by definition, cannot experience death, nor can the dead, by reason of their non-existence, non-consciousness. So why the concern, why the terror?

Though death yields no experience, dying does, and it is generally painful. When death is imminent a rational person, having no fear of death, should seek to shorten the dying period. Particularly might one expect such rational behavior of the religious person who says he has no doubt that something—the soul—is conserved despite death. Paradoxically, experience contradicts expectation. As the Reverend Joseph Fletcher has said, "Curiously, it is the skeptics about immortality who appear to face death more calmly. They seem somehow less inclined to hang on desperately to life at the cost of indescribable and uncreative suffering for themselves and others."[30]

Equally curious is a correlation noted by Logan Pearsall Smith: "Why are happy people not afraid of Death, while the insatiable and the unhappy so abhor that grim feature?"[31] If Smith's observation is true—and from my limited experience I would say it is—it presents us with the paradox that a happy life is more easily renounced than a miserable one. Hallam Tennyson has said as much: "The more you love life and the more you love people and living amongst them, the easier it is for you to leave them in the end."[32] An economist might explain this by saying that when the good life is as common as water it is as little valued, whereas those to whom good days are as rare as diamonds insatiably cling to the possibility (however remote) of enjoying a few more good days. This is a plausible idea, but a hard one to test.

More important is the following consequence of the correlation just postulated. The more maladaptive a culture is, the greater will be the proportion of its citizens who are unhappy and hence the larger the proportion who will resist leaving life, thus increasing the aggregate of unhappiness of the community. And we can be sure that unhappy people who fight off death for themselves will, from a destructive impulse toward consistency, try to keep hap-

pier and more rational people from diminishing *their* suffering
by shortening *their* dying periods. What we have just described is
a striking example of the homeostatic or self-maintaining power
of any culture, even a pathological one. A cynic may remind us
that pathological homeostasis is what we usually refer to as "a
vicious circle."

People differ strikingly in their attitudes toward death. A person enunciating universalized statements about the properties
and significance of death may merely be rationalizing his own pe-
culiarities. I claim no immunity to this charge; I mention it merely
to alert my readers. When emotions are involved it is particularly
essential to read between the lines. Every writer unknowingly
writes between the lines but seldom can he read between his own
lines: that is left for others to do.

Psychoanalysis has given us some small ability to lay bare our
own (hitherto) unconscious rationalizations. Self-analysis requires considerable courage. Most of the time, most of us do
not have this courage. (Let us honor those who do; let us memo-
rialize rare moments of courage.) A clue to our abhorrence of
death is found in the confessions of George Moore, a now little
known novelist of Victorian and Edwardian days:

> One day my father was suddenly called to Ireland. A few days
> after, a telegram came, and my mother read that we were required
> at his bedside. We journeyed over land and sea, and on a bleak
> country road, one winter's evening, a man approached us and I
> heard him say that all was over, that my father was dead. I loved
> my father; I burst into tears; and yet my soul said, "I am glad."
> The thought came unbidden, undesired, and I turned aside,
> shocked at the sight it afforded of my soul.
>
> O, my father, I, who love and reverence nothing else, love and
> reverence thee; thou art the one pure image in my mind, and the
> one true affection that life has not broken or soiled; I remember
> thy voice and thy kind, happy ways. All I have of worldly goods
> and native wit I received from thee—and was it I who was glad?
> No, it was not I; I had no concern in the thought that then fell
> upon me unbidden and undesired; my individual voice can give
> you but praise and loving words, and the voice that said "I am
> glad" was not my voice, but that of the will to live which we

inherit from elemental dust through countless generations. Terrible and imperative is the voice of the will to live: let him who is innocent cast the first stone.

Terrible is the day when each sees his soul naked, stripped of all veil; that dear soul which he cannot change or discard, and which is so irreparably his.

My father's death freed me, and I sprang like a loosened bough up to the light. His death gave me power to create myself, that is to say, to create a complete and absolute self out of the partial self which was all that the restraint of home had permitted; this future self, this ideal George Moore, beckoned me, lured like a ghost; and as I followed the funeral the question, Would I sacrifice this ghostly self, if by so doing I should bring my father back? presented itself without intermission, and I shrank horrified at the answer which I could not crush out of my mind.[33]

Moore was thirty-four years old when he wrote this passage, which was published in the same year—1886—as Robert Louis Stevenson's *The Strange Case of Dr. Jekyll and Mr. Hyde*, and thirteen years before Sigmund Freud's *Interpretation of Dreams*. The Freudian insight was "in the air"; it was an inevitable product of the drive toward naturalism in "fiction," an art form that frequently leads us to truth faster than nonfiction, faster than cautious scholars may care to go.

"My father's death freed me," says Moore. Of what? Of the necessity of competing with the father, in a word, of the burden of the Oedipus complex (not yet named in 1886). "The voice that said 'I am glad' was not my voice," protests Moore, "but that of the will to live which we inherit from elemental dust through countless generations." By assimilating the terrible insight of his own nature into the Darwinian interpretation of all Nature, Moore was able to write down honestly the terror-evoking truth. The social cost of lesser honesty is the enunciation of "compassionate" statements that hypocritically and untruthfully assert that all deaths are evil, that no death has its useful aspects.

In the field of competition, hypocrisy is a useful weapon. By hypocritically echoing John Donne's statement that "any man's death diminishes me" I signal to whom-it-may-concern that I will not compete with him—thus rendering him unprepared for my clandestine competitive cunning. So avid is our hunger for "love" —our word for the noncompetitive attention of others—that we generally accept at face value almost any statement that identifies death as an unmitigated evil. Thus the popular press, a patsy for hypocrisy, constantly grinds out statements like this: "There was a new sorrow in the family of Mrs. John F. Kennedy: her late husband's grandmother, Mrs. Josephine Fitzgerald, died at 98."[34] No evidence is given that the mixed feelings of the family added up to a *net* sum of sorrow; considering the average condition of ninety-eight-year-olds, the burden of proof should certainly fall on those who assert sorrow in such a case. The popular press is trapped in hypocrisy—which it helps perpetuate. Another vicious circle.

More serious is the situation in which the medical profession finds itself. Physicians are the legal gatekeepers standing between life and death. It behooves us to be concerned about the attitudes of these gatekeepers. Their bias as a group is towards life, and we would not have it otherwise: but should the bias be *total*? It is noteworthy that a number of researchers have found that physicians are *more* afraid of death than are their patients or the general populace.[35] It is not, then, surprising that the medical profession so often gives patients what they don't want (prolonged dying) rather than what they do want (a quick and merciful death). This is one of the reasons Ivan Illich caustically identifies modern medicine as one of the "disabling professions."[36] Medicine is aided and abetted, of course, by the legal profession, with its contorted and often counter-productive concern with personal liability.

The unwillingness of physicians to think rationally about death can lead to ridiculous policy proposals. For instance the noted heart-surgeon Dr. Michael DeBakey in 1967 presented this argument for a greatly expanded program of government-supported research in his field: "The need for developing an artificial heart becomes immediately apparent on computing the Nation's toll due to all forms of heart disease—a total of almost a million citizens a year. This outweighs all other causes of death combined, including cancer, infectious diseases, and accidents."[37]

The statistical fallacy embedded in this argument does not require an M.D. degree to spot. A dozen years earlier Hugh Morrison, dealing with a similar problem, wrote:

> The percentages of deaths from all causes must naturally add up to 100. As medical science eliminates one cause of death after another, the percentages must still add up to 100. That is what confuses people. We all must die of something. There is only one way to decrease our percentage of deaths from heart disease, and that is to increase our percentage of deaths from other things. What would you like to have increased? [38]

One is reminded of a would-be humorous French book published two generations ago entitled 21 *Delightful Ways to Commit Suicide*: the ultimate way, resorted to only by those too cowardly to choose from the first twenty, is to die of old age. The twenty-one ways add up to 100 percent of all deaths, of course. Which way will you choose?

Fortunately change is now taking place in the attitude of physicians toward death and dying. Dr. Elisabeth Kübler-Ross's book *On Death and Dying* has been the most influential single work.[39] When Dr. Ross began her investigations at the University of Chicago she was told by staff physicians that they had no dying patients, an unbelievable statement in a great university hospital that attracts difficult medical cases. She had to find her cases by quietly consulting nurses and interns, much to the distress of some staff officers. It was at this point in her investigations that Dr. Ross realized that physicians, when it comes to accepting death, may be more of a problem than their patients.

Thus far the approach to death has been principally oriented by the interests of the individual. This is in keeping with the temper of our time which is predominantly individualistic. Unless the matter is called to our attention we unthinkingly assume that whatever benefits the individual benefits the group. But we know that the individualistic assumption of laissez faire is not, in general, true. It may be to *my* interest that I be allowed to catch whales without restriction, but if everyone acts on this rule whales will soon be extinguished and we will all suffer. Similarly, I may want to live forever, but what if I (and everyone else) could do so?

Let us see what the consequences would be if immortality became natural.

Even with natural immortality accidental deaths would continue to occur. Suppose we assume the low American rate of accidents (about 5 per 10,000 per year) and assume that this rate is un-affected by the age of our immortals. The probability that an individual will survive for one year is $(1-.0005)=0.9995$, and the probability that he will survive for n years is this figure raised to the nth power. The "life expectancy" (50/50 chance) then becomes 1,386 years. Calculations by the demographer Nathan Keyfitz lead to the conclusion that, so far, some 80 billion human beings have been born on earth.[40] Not even the most "optimistic" of cornucopian visionaries assume that the earth can support twenty times the present human population in comfort and dignity, so we must conclude that if an otherwise rational society discovered the secret of immortality it would see to it that births were allowed only to the extent needed to replace deaths (which, by the hypothesis of accidents, would be 5 per 10,000 per year in our Brave New World). The equilibrium birth rate of 5 per 10,000 should be compared with the present U.S. rate of 150 per 10,000, and a typical rate for a contemporary poor country, namely 450 per 10,000 per year. Birth in a society of immortals would be so rare as to justify selling tickets to witness the event.

Such a low birth rate would lead to some interesting consequences. If our ancestors had achieved immortality and created a zero population growth society a long, long time ago, then 50 percent of our present population would have been born before 593 A.D., and could be expected to remember most of the career of Mohammed. Some 10 percent of the population would have been born before 2625 B.C.: they should remember King Tut, the fall of Troy, and all subsequent Greek and Roman history. Twenty-eight percent would remember the birth of Buddha, and 37 percent the birth of Christ. (I assume no senile decay of memory.)

At the present time one person out of four in a rich country is less than fifteen years old; in poor countries the proportion is nearly one out of two. In our hypothetical population of immortals the proportion of children would be one out of 134. Infants and children would be a rarity. But since, by hypothesis, the adults would be youthfully vigorous, would it matter? I think it would. For one thing, contact with the young is marvelously educational, as every parent can testify. In El Dorado few would be able to partake of this education. The statistical effect would be exacerbated by the repressive effect of the predominance of mature people, 134 to one. In such a society it is doubtful if children would act much like children, not the children we know. Something precious would be lost.

In addition, what would life be like for the adults? Work is an important part of our lives, and the conditions of work matter. In large groups the only satisfactory way to organize the work force is in a hierarchy. The larger the organization the more essential hierarchy is. Were human beings utterly without feelings of envy it might be possible to arrange the hierarchy by merit alone. But since envy is a central fact of life we generally allow seniority great, and sometimes predominant, importance in determining each person's position. There can be only a few persons at the top. In a society in which more than half the people were more than 1,300 years old how long would an ambitious business person have to wait before becoming vice-president of his firm? Ten thousand years? What would he do in the meantime? Stir up trouble? Ten thousand years of trouble?

Another difficulty is plausible but hardly provable. Granted that there would be no physiological aging in El Dorado, it does not follow that the individual mind would escape changing in such a way as to mimic some of the changes we now attribute to aging. If Aristotle were still alive, dare we assume that his character would have been changed, on the whole, for the better by his twenty-three centuries of experience? What effect would it have on a person to live through so many centuries of social revolution and political upset? Would the experience make him wiser, more understanding? Or would the information overload turn him into a sort of Hamlet, incapable of decisive action?

We don't know; but neither do we have any reason for optimism. Worn-out individuals take up precious space in society, but so also would individuals who were not worn-out, if they lived forever. Even on the individualistic level, there is not much to be said in favor of immortality. Rip Van Winkle wasn't very happy when he woke into a new world after twenty years; I see no reason to think that Aristotle would be happy living through twenty-three centuries.

As for society, who needs Aristotle forever? We have done well enough without him. Genius, rare as it is, is in over-supply; it is the environment in which genius can flourish that is hardest to come by. In his *Elegy in a Country Church-Yard* Thomas Gray remarked that in a remote rural environment, "Full many a flower is born to blush unseen." This is no doubt true: a critical mass of population may be necessary for the nurturing of certain sorts of excellence. But beyond some optimum population size, friction between individuals and the necessities of hierarchy insure that proportionately more and more "mute, inglorious Miltons" will live out their lives without realizing the potentialities of their genius. England today is twelve times more populous than it was in Milton's day: does it have twelve times as many Miltons?

However much the individual may wish to live forever—and I submit that few healthy, happy individuals do want to live forever—no carefully reasoned argument has ever been presented for the social value of immortality. Yet we spend fantastic sums of money in research on the diseases of old age, and there is a steady stream of promises of El Dorado some day. The generalized defense of such expenditure is soft-headed: "They laughed at Jules Verne, and look at us now! Who is to say what the limits of technological ingenuity are?" Though it refers to the future this argument cannot lay claim to foresight. What are at issue are not the scientific possibilities, but the political and social possibilities. We would be mad to finance a line of research as flagrantly Epimethean as research aimed at achieving immortality, or even a very long life. There comes a time when death is better—for the individual and for society. When we fully realize this we will insist that no geriatric research be supported with federal funds unless an Environmental Impact Study (EIS) has demonstrated that the research, if successful, will be of *social* value. In general, this means that the aim of the research must be to increase the vigor of people in their declining years without increasing their longevity. If these two kinds of "benefits" cannot be separated in practice, we may decide that the research should not be done at all. This is a Promethean possibility. The Promethean discipline of the EIS, created to deal with the environment external to human beings, needs to be applied to the internal environment of society.

Chapter III

Competition

Competition, said Samuel Johnson in the first great dictionary of the English language (1755), is "the action of endeavouring to gain what another endeavours to gain at the same time." The verb "endeavour" gives the definition an anthropomorphic cast which (as has happened with so many words) has now been outgrown in technical usage. Scientists speak not only of the competition of men, wolves, and lemmings (all of which, perhaps, endeavor or strive, psychologically speaking), but also of the competition of grasses and even of enzymes, which certainly have no psychological impulses. As far as concerns the consequences of competition, the consciousness behind the action is irrelevant. It is the process that matters.

Ecologists distinguish competition from such other forms of conflict as predation and parasitism. A gazelle and a zebra may compete for the same kind of grass, but the lion that preys on the grass-eaters is usually spoken of as a predator rather than a competitor. However, there is a deeper sense in which lion and gazelle are competitors. The great theoretical physicist Ludwig Boltzmann (1844–1906) remarked that "the struggle for existence is the struggle for free energy," that is, for the low-entropy energy that comes to us from the sun. In this sense all living things may be said to compete with each other. (Competition does not preclude a measure of cooperation.) For the most part I shall hereafter use the word "competition" in this larger sense to deal with many examples of the "struggle for existence."

The idea of competition, like the idea of death, is something that some people can face easily and others cannot. Biologists have no difficulty with it, neither do businessmen or politicians (in their private moments—in public, they often disparage competition, making a great show of calling for cooperation). It is only when we move into the academic world that we find a sizable body of people who clearly are disturbed by the idea of competition. We are not surprised to note that young people whose needs are taken care of by their elders often fail to appreciate the inevitability of competition. What is surprising is that adults whose specialty is the behavior of human beings in groups—sociologists —should hold competition in such low esteem. A large contingent of sociologists regards competition in the human species as either unnecessary, wicked, or both. A survey[1] of twenty modern textbooks in elementary sociology found that seven did not even mention the word. The average text had only one in 222 of its pages indexed under "competition"; in some cases the passage cited consisted of a single deprecatory sentence. The phenomenon of competition, if acknowledged at all, was discussed as an evil. The following passage from the Bergers' *Sociology* gives the flavor of this literature:

> The educational system not only fosters competition but (except in some sports) *individual* competition. Each individual competes with all others. The academic sin of "cheating" brings this feature out very clearly. To give help to a weaker peer in an examination is defined and morally reproved as "cheating" in American education; in another society (and, indeed, sometimes in the sub-society of the peer group even in America) the same act may be defined as an expression of "friendship," and morally approved or even required as such. A further refinement of this particular definition of the situation is the so-called "honor system," still operating in many schools and colleges. Here, the individual is not only not supposed to "cheat" but to keep an eye on all others to make sure that *they* don't—and to report them to the proper authorities in case they do. All of this expresses a morality both competitive and individualistic, and by the same token discouraging of such solidarity between individuals that would impede successful achievement in the system by each of them.[2]

Setting aside the ambiguity of the unhappy last sentence, we can generously credit the authors with compassion, but it is an Epimethean compassion only. They have not asked the Promethean question *And then what?* What would the educational system produce if we saw to it that competitive excellence was not rewarded? Suppose we should decide to eliminate individualistic competition among our medical students, permitting them to practice the virtue of "solidarity" whenever they take examinations? Suppose we create two classes of medical schools, one of which is the individualistically competitive sort we have now, and the other a noncompetitive, solidarity-serving sort in which failure is impossible. Let the graduates of the two types of schools be clearly labeled in the telephone directory and on the brass plates at their doors. ("Competitive M.D." and "Solidarity M.D." would do.) Then let sociologists choose their *personal* physicians—while the rest of us watch with keen interest!

I think sociologists belittle the importance of competition in academic studies because they don't regard the studies themselves as of any importance. In some areas of academia I daresay they are right.

Since competition is perceived as standing in opposition to co-operation some people seem to assume that those who can look without flinching at the process of competition must be, by nature, brutal. It is therefore of interest to note the character of Charles Darwin, the man who set competition in the very center of biological theory. His century—the nineteenth—was one that saw the triumph of a value-system to which the general label "humanitarianism" is given. The "best people" committed themselves to deal fairly and compassionately with slaves, animals, children, and women (in that historical sequence!). Charles Darwin, a child of his century, was a notably compassionate man. As a youth he gave up the study of medicine because he could not bear to witness surgical operations. He said, of two very bad operations that he saw at Edinburgh, that they "fairly haunted me for many a long year." As an adult, though a shy man, he would intervene in any public mistreatment of horses, dogs, or children. The mere thought of cruelty often robbed him of sleep.

Yet this was the man who, in his *Origin of Species*, firmly established the inescapability of the "struggle for existence," a term which (he said), "I use . . . in a large and metaphorical sense."[3] More than a decade before the *Origin*, Alfred Tennyson had spoken of "Nature, red in tooth and claw,"[4] overemphasizing an impression that does not arise directly and necessarily from long continued, close observation of animals and plants in the wild. For dramatic purposes bloody conflict is selectively given the place of honor in adventure stories (and, in our day, in nature movies and television shows), but he who spends many days watching nature at work and at play seldom witnesses a bloody encounter. Those he does see are soon over. However, the thoughtful observer ultimately transcends a merely statistical view of reality to reach a conclusion not unlike the poet's, though the resemblance is more in the theoretical realm than in the visual:

> Nothing is easier than to admit in words the truth of the universal struggle for life, or more difficult—at least I found it so—than constantly to bear this conclusion in mind. Yet unless it be thoroughly engrained in the mind, the whole economy of nature, with every fact on distribution, rarity, abundance, extinction, and variation, will be dimly seen or quite misunderstood. We behold the face of nature bright with gladness, we often see superabundance of food; we do not see or we forget that the birds which are idly singing round us mostly live on insects or seeds, and are thus constantly destroying life; or we forget how largely these songsters, or their eggs, or their nestlings, are destroyed by birds and beasts of prey. . . .[5]

Such is Darwin's warning. He goes on to say that we must

> . . . keep steadily in mind that each organic being is striving to increase in a geometrical ratio; that each, at some period of its life, during some season of the year, during each generation, or at intervals, has to struggle for life and to suffer great destruction. When we reflect on this struggle we may console ourselves with the full belief that the war of nature is not incessant, that no fear is felt, that death is generally prompt, and that the vigorous, the healthy and the happy survive and multiply.[6]

These are the words of a man who is both compassionate and thoughtful. In Aristotelian language, bloodiness (when it exists) is only an *accident* of competition, not its *essence*. Many of Darwin's studies were carried out with overcrowded plant seedlings,

among which competition is unspectacular and quite unbloody—
and most effective. What really matters in evolution is not the
means but the final result—which is the same everywhere, "the
survival of the fittest," to use Herbert Spencer's journalistic simplification. And we must never lose sight of the fact that the
survival of the fittest is a statistical truth only, with many individual exceptions.

For each species at each moment the result of competition is the
survival of the fittest, but for the living world as a whole there is
also a "final" result, namely the establishment of a great bio-
sphere, with its millions of species interacting with each other in
a complexity of ways far beyond our certain knowledge, producing a world whose beauty we could never have imagined, had we
been present at the beginning when the simplest form of life first
appeared, about three billion years ago. Overwhelmed with the
mysterious beauty of it all, Darwin concluded the *Origin* with this
peroration:

> It is interesting to contemplate a tangled bank, clothed with
> many plants of many kinds, with birds singing on the bushes,
> with various insects flitting about, and with worms crawling
> through the damp earth, and to reflect that these elaborately con-
> structed forms, so different from each other, and dependent upon
> each other in so complex a manner, have all been produced by
> laws acting around us. These laws, taken in the largest sense,
> being Growth with reproduction; Inheritance which is almost im-
> plied by reproduction; Variability from the indirect and direct
> action of the conditions of life, and from use and disuse; a Ratio
> of Increase so high as to lead to a Struggle for Life; and as a con-
> sequence to Natural Selection, entailing Divergence of Character
> and the Extinction of less improved forms. Thus, *from the war
> of nature, from famine and death, the most exalted object which
> we are capable of conceiving, namely, the production of the high-
> er animals, directly follows.* There is grandeur in this view of life,
> with its several powers, having been originally breathed by the
> Creator into a few forms or into one; and that, while this planet
> has gone circling on according to the fixed law of gravity, from
> so simple a beginning endless forms most beautiful and most
> wonderful have been and are being evolved.[7]

The italicization above is intended to call attention to the fact that the apparently ugly processes of competition can lead to great beauty. Is this an Aristotelian accident, or is it of the essence of competition?

Beauty may or may not be a consequence of biological competition, but variety certainly is. Let us first consider the problem of stability in a species before looking for the mechanism that produces change. In adopting this order we follow the historical sequence of the development of evolutionary theory. The first steps were taken in 1835 by a nearly forgotten English naturalist, Edward Blyth.[8] The essence of his argument will be expanded and translated into biological terms that came much later.[9]

What we are is determined by the genes we inherit, their action being modified by the environment. For a variety of technical reasons it is difficult to say exactly how many different genes are required to make up a human being but the number 100,000 will do. One may think of these genes as positions (*loci* is the technical term) on the genetic information map; at each locus, any of a large number of chemical "words" can be set. Of the many potential chemical words at each position only a tiny fraction (sometimes only one word) is compatible with life. The great variety of human beings is accounted for by only a limited variation in genes at a tiny fraction of the genetic loci. Most conceivable changes are not compatible with life.

The chemical-genetic material is unstable. Every gene can mutate from one form to a number of others. In part, mutations are caused by controllable influences like X-radiation and mutagenic chemicals like mustard gas. In addition, inescapable cosmic rays cause mutations. Beyond this, mutations may be attributable to a residual, intrinsic, chemical instability. In a species that is well adapted to its environment the vast majority of the mutations make their possessors less well adapted. The worst of the mutations kill their possessors during gamete formation or during embryological development (resulting, in mammals, in spontaneous abortion). Mutants that are not quite so bad permit the possessors to develop but put them at a disadvantage in competing with more normal types. As a result of competition unfavorable mutants, as a group, leave fewer descendants than the favorable types they compete with. Such differential survival is rhetorically attributed to "natural selection," which is clearly a metaphor.

What if there were no selection? In such case, mutants would not be eliminated. The genetic message would be indefinitely degraded by the disorderly process of repeated mutation. One can think of the genetic message as something like the message in a printed play of Shakespeare's. To reproduce this message we could have a typesetter set up new type from an old copy of the play. In normal practice any mistakes the typesetter makes are caught by the proofreader, whose activities can be thought of as "natural selection." If there is no proofreader—no natural selection—mistakes will accumulate as new errors are committed at each new setting of the type. (The chance that a second mistake will correct an earlier one is very small, and can be ignored.) After many generations (typesettings in series) without natural selection (proofreading) the message would have degenerated beyond recognition, and there would be so little unity among the descendants that one could not even speak of a species.

A little thought shows that this possibility is so highly theoretical that we can hardly imagine it. Competition *is* inescapable, and its primary effect is to keep the variation of a species within rather narrow bounds, thus maintaining stability. Because of inescapable mutation, natural selection is required to preserve stability.

Change in a species comes about when the environment changes thus changing the selective criteria. (To continue our analogy, it is as though new scholarship—environmental pressures—convinced typesetters that the line from *Romeo and Juliet* that runs "A plague o' both your houses!" should really read, "A plague take both your houses!") It is the reality of environmental change that converts the stability-maintaining property of natural selection into a change-producing force. This is no paradox; natural selection is basically ambivalent. Whatever one may regard as the most "exalted" creatures (to use Darwin's term) these organisms owe both their origin and their perpetuation to competition and selection.

In competition some win, some lose. "To be an Error and to be cast out is a part of God's Design," said William Blake, and only a foolishly compassionate Epimethean would want to put an end to the casting out. But, in her own quaint way, nature can be compassionate without violating Promethean precepts. Bloodshed and death are not *required* for the casting out: only diminished reproduction is. The male songbird that loses in the competitive battle is not killed: it is merely exiled to the boondocks where, possessing no ravishing real estate with which to tempt a female, the losing male perforce lives in celibate simplicity.[10] Cruelty and sadism play a vanishingly small role in the drama of nature for this simple, pragmatic reason: they have no selective value.

In fact, natural selection favors behavior that avoids bloody confrontations and vindictive behavior, for even the winner of a bloody encounter stands to lose something if he persists in looking for fights. Fighting machines wear out. "Nature" knows this, and is clever more often than cruel. A thousand anecdotes attest to this: I retell only one, the story of the piratical penis of the damselfly.[11]

Damselflies are dainty, ladylike versions of dragonflies, but the daintiness of the male in love-making is rather curious. In mating, the male deposits a load of sperm into a storage pouch of the female. When the time for laying eggs arrives the female draws on this store to fertilize the eggs. Obviously there is competition among the males to furnish the sperm used for fertilization, and this competition has selected for an interesting variation in the function of the penis. Before depositing his sperm the male uses his intromittent organ as a scraping tool to clear the pouch of the female of any sperms left there by an earlier male; following this evacuation the new male makes his own deposit. No battle, no bloodshed—just surgically clean competitive effectiveness.

So far the discussion has revolved around intraspecific competition. For simplicity in developing the fundamental theory of competition I pass now to a consideration of competition between species (though the principles, once developed, also apply, given certain modifications, to intraspecific competition). I will present this theory in a dialectical fashion, showing first the destructive side before taking up the creative aspects of competition.

When two very similar but non-interbreeding species are brought together in the same habitat the outcome of their competition can be summarized in the "competitive exclusion principle" which can be simply put in four words: *Complete competitors cannot coexist.*[12] If two different species occupy *exactly* the same "ecological niche"—that is, eat the same food, are active at the same time of the day, etc.—then they cannot indefinitely live together in the same (finite) territory because the more efficient species will eventually displace the less efficient.

This principle, about which there is now no serious doubt, had a prolonged birth. Simplifying its history we may say that the idea was first stated with full explicitness in 1944, but was not named until fifteen years later, during the centennial celebrations of Darwin's *Origin of Species* in 1959.[13] Yet excellent traces of the idea can be found forty-four and fifty-five years before it was christened; and, indeed, the idea is demonstrably implicit in the *Origin* itself.

The theory of competitive exclusion is mathematically rigorous.[14] I will give two verbal translations of it, the first brief and close to the mathematical equations, the second wordier and more intuitive.

First we begin with the Malthusian idea that under unchanging environmental conditions every species multiplies exponentially. ("Unchanging conditions" is an abstraction from reality, of course.) For each species in each environment there is a characteristic exponent for the growth equation. In the real world it is inconceivable that any two exponents are *exactly* equal (this is called the *Axiom of Inequality*). The ratio of two exponential functions is itself an exponential function (and, because of the Axiom of Inequality, this exponent is *not* zero). Therefore, in the course of time, one species will completely displace the other. Q.E.D.

Now for the wordier version.

Let us imagine a very odd savings bank which has only two depositors. For some obscure reason the bank pays one of the depositors 2 percent compound interest, while paying the other 2.01 percent. Let us suppose further (and here the analogy is really strained) that whenever the sum of the combined funds of the two depositors reaches two million dollars the bank arbitrarily appropriates one million dollars of it, taking from each depositor in proportion to his holdings at that time. Then both accounts are allowed to grow until their sum again equals two million dollars, at which time the appropriation process is repeated. If this procedure is continued indefinitely, what will happen to the wealth of these two depositors? A little intuition shows us (and mathematics verifies) that the man who receives the greater rate of interest will, in time, have *all* the money, and the other man none (we assume a penny cannot be subdivided). No matter how small the difference between the two interest rates (so long as there is a difference) such will be the outcome.

Translated into evolutionary terms, that is what competition in nature amounts to. The fluctuating limit of one million to two million represents the finite available wealth (food, shelter, etc.) of any natural environment, and the difference in interest rates represents the difference between the competing species in their efficiency in producing offspring. No matter how small this difference may be, one species will eventually replace the other. In the scale of geological time, even a small competitive difference will result in a rapid extermination of the less successful species. Competitive differences that are so small as to be unmeasurable by direct means will, by virtue of the compound-interest effect, ultimately result in the extinction of one competing species by another.[15]

The logic of the principle is compelling. *How could it be otherwise?* We see no useful way to doubt it. But the principle is only part of the total ecological theory of populations. It does not operate in a vacuum, any more than Newton's first law of motion does. This principle *plus others* determines what actually happens. Operating by itself, the exclusion principle would surely make for a poorer world in the sense that its variety would diminish.[16] In fact, however, competition acting in consort with other principles, actually has a creative effect: it increases the variety of the living world. One of the important subsidiary principles is that of "ecological succession," as illustrated by the following example.

Crush some ripe grapes and put them in a large, open vat. What happens? The bulk of the sugary liquid soon becomes anaerobic, favoring the growth of yeast cells over all other species. The yeast cells use up the sugar, turning it into alcohol. At the peak of their growth yeast cells vastly outnumber the cells of other species. But, in exploiting the environment the yeast cells ruin it—for themselves. Alcohol, the waste product of their metabolism, is poisonous to them. Most of the yeast cells die. Then, if oxygen can enter from the surface of the vat, the oxygen-requiring acetic acid bacteria take over and turn alcohol into acetic acid. (Thus is hard cider turned into vinegar.) If oxygen continues to be available, a variety of microbial species will later metabolize the acid to carbon dioxide and water. Is that the end of the process? Not quite: the various microbial cells, running out of food, finally die, releasing their body-chemicals into the liquid to serve as food for yet other microbes.

Ecological succession depends on the fact that each species, by its success, tends to destroy the conditions that enabled it to become successful. In the strictest meaning of the word "tragic"— the Greek meaning—we can say that ecological succession rests on a tragic fact. Tragic, but not sad—not for us, the observers and potential exploiters of the tragedy. By controlling the tragic process we can increase or decrease the amounts of the end-products, producing dry wines, sweet wines, vinegar, or complete destruction of the organic matter, as we wish.

If the competitive exclusion principle were the only principle of ecology, the world would be very simple. But it isn't: ecological succession makes the world richer. The waste products of one species create one or more ecological niches—opportunities—for other species. Competition creates environmental fragmentation, and the fragmentation creates a richer world.

Evolution also enters into the picture. Each species has the capability of living in several environments that are at least slightly different. If a new competitor—an immigrant species—displaces a species from one of its niches the displaced species may still be able to survive in another. Species survival then depends on the mutation-and-selection that takes place in the alternate environment: competition between species creates a selection that favors ecological differentiation. Survival, then, can take place either by victory or by differentiation. More often than not (and somewhat paradoxically) competition favors an escape from competition. In biology, survival is the supreme value. The exclusion principle can be restated: *ecological differentiation is the necessary condition for coexistence.*

Though these examples have been drawn from the nonhuman world, the reader must surely have been stimulated to think of human analogues. In the commercial world, product differentiation is functionally the same as ecological differentiation. The waste products of one industry are the raw materials of another (niche multiplication). The success of television, for example, created a niche for the *TV Guide*, which made its promoter rich, eventually sending him to the Court of St. James.

I said that ecological succession is a tragic event in the Greek sense because success undermines the conditions of success. This tragic idea is immensely older than ecology; it can, in fact, be traced back at least to Plato with his description of the natural succession of governments: aristocracy → timocracy → oligarchy → democracy → anarchy → tyranny → back to aristocracy. Each type of government, by its success, tragically changes the cultural conditions so as to favor the next one in the series. In the words of an obscure nineteenth-century writer, Piercy Ravenstone, "Every society, from its first formation, bears in its bosom the seeds of its destruction."[17] One could hardly ask for a pithier statement of the tragedy of ecological succession.

Can we escape developmental tragedy in the human realm? Every vigorous human society, whatever its political stage of the moment, thinks it can. Adolf Hitler spoke of the "Thousand Year Reich"—which lasted ten. Other political leaders are only slightly less ridiculous. When some nation has succeeded in stopping the succession for, say, fifty generations, perhaps such a claim can be taken seriously. (Though we should not fail to ask, at what cost is political stability achieved?) The possibility of long-term stability is clearly a central question for political science.

Enough of praise for competition: now we must ask, Can we have too much of this good thing? Of course we can. We need to investigate the limits of competition as a melioristic process, if we are to guard against pejoristic backlash.[18] The principle "too much of a good thing" applies to politics because *power breeds power*. As an engineer would put it, political power is a force with "positive feedback." Perhaps "in nature"—i.e., in the nonhuman world—positive feedback is nothing to worry about. The male wolf that is only a little better than others in the pack is accorded exclusive breeding rights to the females. This may not be "fair," but it cannot be argued that it harms either the pack or the species.

Turning to human beings we soon discover the paradox that *power has the power to destroy the freedom that permits it to come into being.* This is a reality that staggers our imagination, causing us to doubt the conventional wisdom that clusters around the words "tolerance" and "freedom."

It is astonishing how many elements enter into the positive feedback of power in human systems. Capital can be accumulated as we pay interest on capital; compound interest is a form of positive feedback—interest becomes capital which earns interest which becomes capital which . . . and so on, without *intrinsic* limit. The accumulation of capital can transcend the gaps between generations. With enough capital one can buy an escape from the rules that govern those who have no capital. It is no wonder that the ancient Hebrews forbade "usury," by which they meant the taking of interest on money loaned. (The proscription applied only on transactions between "brothers," not between strangers!)[19] We may yet, as John Maynard Keynes speculated in 1930, return to the ancient Hebrew ideal.[20]

The power of advertising and the media is probably the greatest threat of all to freedom in our time. With money, information can be suppressed, rumors magnified, and meaning obscured under an information overload that is created in the name of objectivity. Many years ago Walter Lippmann made a comment about newspaper publishers that now applies with at least equal force to television programmers: "The power to determine each day what shall seem important and what shall be neglected is a power unlike any that has been exercised since the Pope lost his hold on the secular mind."[21]

Classical economics of the Smith-Ricardian type sees competition as almost wholly good and inherently productive of stability, yet the experience of thousands of years denies that utterly free competition produces a steady state. In the limited context of economics, the Platonic ecological succession must read something like this: completely free enterprise → oligopoly → monopoly → economic tyranny → economic revolution → economic anarchy

→ mercantilism → return to free enterprise. This equation is not the established wisdom, but it should be a useful hypothesis for further research. Ecological succession, part of the dialectic of competition, needs to be taken seriously. The costs of allowing it, and the costs of preventing it—if it can be prevented—need to be known.

There is a more pressing threat to humanity, the discussion of which is largely repressed at the present time. I shall risk breaking the taboo. The issue is this: shall we tolerate the use of breeding power as a weapon in the competition between nations? Whether such use is deliberate or not, political power is influenced by population and population growth in many areas of the globe. I shall deal with only one instance. The insights derived from this analysis are (with suitable modifications) applicable to other areas.

The instance is the Near East. Arbitrarily neglecting the earlier history of the region and the peoples living there we can say that there has been no stable peace for the nation of Israel since its founding in 1948. Part of the instability can be attributed to errors or injustices committed in the formation of Israel, e.g., the displacement of Palestinian non-Jews. But it would be a mistake to suppose that only such particularities are at the bottom of the present trouble.

As a thought-experiment, imagine yourself with dictatorial powers: turn the clock back to 1948 and try to devise some other scheme for creating a Jewish state in the Near East without displacing or harming any of the people living there. There is no way to do it. Once the powerful states outside the region were committed to creating Israel they were committed to the creation of an insoluble problem, given the semi-humanitarian restraints of modern international politics. And however hopeless the situation was in 1948, it has grown steadily more hopeless. Why? Because the great nations that seek to impose peace from the outside will not face the reality and the consequences of the competition in breeding that makes the objective situation of the Israeli ever worse.

The Jews of Israel are a minority in their part of the world. As of 1978 the population of Israel was 3.7 million, of whom 85 percent, or 3.1 million, were Jews. The minority in this nation, most of whom are Moslems, do not make for internal stability. Worse, however, are the external demographic threats. The Moslems of the surrounding countries vastly outnumber the Jews of Israel. If only the near countries (including Egypt) are counted, Moslems outnumber Jews in the region by twenty to one; if one includes more distant countries, out to Morocco, Moslems outnumber Jews forty to one.

If present trends continue this inequality will steadily increase. The population of Israel is growing at 2.2 percent per year,[22] while the growth rate of the surrounding Moslems is about 3.4 percent per year. Such is the power of compound interest that this difference in growth rate will, if continued for thirty years, increase the size of the larger Moslem population by 173 percent, while the smaller Jewish population grows by only 92 percent. The 20-to-1 ratio of Moslems-to-Jews becomes, in one generation, a ratio of 28-to-1. In terms of demographic factors, however poor may be the prospects for the peaceful survival of Israel at this time, they can only become worse in the future. Anyone who cherishes the contributions of Jews to Western civilization cannot but view the future of Israel with alarm.

The competitive exclusion principle is working toward the elimination of Jews in the Moslem-Jewish world. This is a contingent truth, not a necessary one. If each nation were a well isolated unit, with the principal interaction between nations that of peaceful trade, then the greater rate of reproduction of the Moslems might actually disadvantage them, for a poor nation cannot afford modern armaments. Overbreeding reduces the military threat of a poor nation to others. Moreover such a nation is in danger of breeding itself into ecological disaster and a "population crash," following which it would be no military threat at all to its neighbors. (It might, however, be a "charitable threat," but that possibility depends on the survivor-nation.)

The twentieth century has seen the rise of sentiments that interfere with automatic, intrinsic correctives to overbreeding. Two "universal human rights" have been asserted which, taken together, spell disaster. The first, in the language of the United Nations, describes "the family as the natural and fundamental unit of society. It follows that any choice and decision with regard to the size of the family must irrevocably rest with the family itself, and cannot be made by anyone else."[23] If a nation refuses to interfere with the breeding behavior of its own families, no other nation or group can.

The second "universal human right" now being asserted is variously called "the right to freedom from hunger," "the right to food," or "the right to good health"—in a word, the right to continued life, which is presumed to include all the normal functions of life including unhindered breeding.

From an Epimethean point of view one cannot fault the ethics of either of these asserted rights. If *Thou* elect to have a child, and then ask me for food for that child, how can *I* refuse? But changing the scale from one *Thou* to 50 million *Thous*, and taking account of the future needs of posterity, changes the problem and calls for a Promethean approach. If everyone who wants to have a child has the right to have as many as he (she) wants, but does not have the responsibility of keeping the child alive—if this responsibility falls on the rest of the world (which did not breed the child), disaster follows. The formula for disaster is simple:

Right to Breed + Right to Food → Breeding War

In a finite world—and no other is available to us—a breeding war works toward the competitive exclusion of the slower breeding group.

This fact has not, I think, escaped the attention of the leaders of the Moslem world. Of course we should not expect to find a Moslem leader saying publicly to the Jews, "We are going to outbreed you," for such an announcement would risk provoking counter-measures. But consider the implications of the statement made by the Egyptian foreign minister in 1974 that peace in the Near East would require Israel "not to increase the number of its immigrants for the next fifty years."[24]

A population may be increased by either immigration or births; the effect, as far as the competitive exclusion principle is concerned, is the same. Increase is increase. It is easy to see why the Egyptian minister did not mention births. Egypt has a birth rate of thirty-nine per thousand and a death rate of thirteen per thousand, yielding a natural increase of twenty-six per thousand, or 2.6 percent per year. Israel, by contrast, shows corresponding rates of twenty-eight and seven respectively, producing a natural increase of 2.1 percent per year. It is not to Egypt's interest to mention this breeding difference. But it was safe for the Egyptian minister to focus on migration, for Egypt probably has a net out-migration, whereas Israel clearly has a sizable in-migration.

An effective defensive strategy for Israel might be to raise the breeding issue. *But no Israeli does.* Why not? Why the taboo? I think we know the answer.

If an Israeli urged that the Moslem populations cut down their breeding he would be accused of promoting genocide. The modern state of Israel is to a large extent the creation of Jews who fled from genocide. No Israeli dares raise the breeding issue in public. Perhaps none can even think of it in the privacy of his own mind, though repressing the thought may be fatal.

In the meantime a state like Egypt, eleven times the size of Israel, continues to produce babies at a rate that is thirty-nine times faster than that of the Jews in Israel. Neither nation is capable of feeding all its own people; U.S. foreign aid supplies 10 percent of Egypt's GNP, and 18 percent of Israel's.[25] Both countries use some of their aid money to pay for imported food. The outside world, in the name of the Right to Food, keeps an ever larger percentage of the people of such countries alive, oblivious to the Promethean consequences of the well-meant Epimethean charity.

Having raised the taboo-afflicted topic of genocide I feel I should discuss this mode of competition fully. The concept of genocide is not as simple as most newspaper readers suppose. Built into the term is a dangerous ambiguity. Unless this danger is exposed we may drift into making harmful decisions.

"Genocide" is a new word: it is not found in the great *Oxford English Dictionary* of 1933. It is a hybrid made up of the Greek *genos*, meaning race or people, coupled with the Latin suffix *cide*, meaning cut or kill. Genocide is, then, the killing of a people. Is this a substantive definition or a metaphor?

In 1948 the General Assembly of the United Nations defined genocide as:

any of the following acts committed with intent to destroy, in whole or in part, a national, ethnical, racial or religious group, as such:

(a) Killing members of the group;
(b) Causing serious bodily or mental harm to members of the group;
(c) Deliberately inflicting on the group conditions of life calculated to bring about its physical destruction in whole or in part;
(d) Imposing measures intended to prevent births within the group;
(e) Forcibly transferring children of the group to another group.[26]

Certainly item (a) above deserves to be called genocide: the most blatant example of our day is the killing of six million Jews by the Nazis.[27] But we must question the labeling of birth prevention (d) as an act of killing. When births are reduced from forty per thousand per year to fifteen, is it correct to say that this takes place through the murder of twenty-five per thousand per year? The suffix *-cide* means murder (or at least, homicide). Note that we do not equate voluntary celibacy with suicide; neither do we call involuntary celibacy (with its consequent infertility) homicide, though we inflict it on prisoners. The nonappearance of potential members of another generation surely has a different moral significance than the violent elimination of existing members of the present generation. Saying that birth prevention is genocide is not fact but metaphor.

But: this is not to say that the act of preventing births is without ethical significance. Certainly it has *bio*ethical significance. In the long-term history of any species or group the prevention of reproduction can play a more important role than violent death. Biologists have been proclaiming this ever since the *Origin of Species*. Using Blake's language, we may say that in the final result, "casting out" matters more than bloodshed. Denying the propriety of calling birth prevention "genocide" does not belittle its moral importance. But in the breeding competition of nations, *the prevention of births is only half the repertoire: the other half is augmentation.* Augmentation has precisely the same effect as diminution, but with a reversal in the roles of victor and vanquished.

The proper analytical vehicle for the ethical investigation of nonbloody competition is not the metaphor of genocide but the principle of competitive exclusion. The point is easily illustrated.

Suppose two competing populations, A and B, have each a fertility rate of forty per thousand per year, and "all other things are equal." If A seeks to eliminate B by breeding how might it do so? Obviously by forcing (or persuading) B to drop its fertility to a rate below forty, while A keeps its fertility rate unchanged. But A can achieve the same result just as surely by leaving B's rate unchanged while increasing its own fertility to, say forty-five. Either policy, indefinitely continued, will eventually eliminate group B.

The United Nations calls the first method genocide; it never calls the second method anything—in fact, it never even mentions it. Hardly anybody mentions it. And nobody listens to those who do. Yet the logic of the competitive exclusion principle tells us that one policy is as deserving of the name "genocide" as the other. At the present moment in history only one policy constitutes "a clear and present danger" to international peace, and that is the policy of encouraging high fertility among one's own group, while insisting on the "Right to Life," which is the modern equivalent of the *Lebensraum* excuse for aggressive national demands.

It is not the absolute level of fertility that matters, but the relative levels of fertility in competing populations. Conventional moral discourse is curiously asymmetrical in its treatment of the facts. The defenders of "rights" cry "Genocide!" when some group asks its too fertile competitors to lower their fertility, but they are silent when any group insists on maintaining its high fertility. The tactical advantage sought through this asymmetry is obvious. Perhaps this behavior also has its source in a persistence of the traditional assumption that all life is good, that more life is better than less. We are reluctant to ask whether we may not be threatened by too much of this good thing, life. The asymmetrical taboo on our thinking, unless it can be dissolved, insures tragedy in the long run.

In the advancement of science the importance of expensive apparatus and clever logical analysis has been adequately publicized. What has not been sufficiently emphasized are those two rules for making fundamental advances in theory:

Take a simple idea;
and take it seriously.

Malthus, in the third chapter of *An Essay on the Principle of Population*, introduced the phrase "the struggle for existence," using it only once in a rather superficial way before passing on to other matters. Forty years later Darwin, happening to read Malthus "for amusement," was "at once struck" with the idea that the struggle for existence explained how "favorable variations would tend to be preserved, and unfavourable ones to be destroyed. . . . Here, then I had at last got a theory by which to work."[28] Here was the simple idea that Darwin took so seriously that he accumulated, and evaluated, the facts that bore on it for another twenty years before permitting himself to publish, in 1858, a brief presentation of his theory to be followed by his great book the following year. A total of sixty-one years elapsed from Malthus' casual mention of the struggle for existence to the full-scale working out of the biological consequences of competition in the *Origin of Species*.

It took courage for Darwin to investigate the consequences of the struggle for existence in the biological realm. It will take equal or greater courage to explore the consequences of competition in the specifically human part of the world. Human beings are not only subject to rules of competition, they can also make many of the rules. Some of these rules they call "rights." (To call them mere "rules" would make them more vulnerable to doubt; rhetorical deception is an important element of competitive tactics.) Every invention of a right is a ploy in the struggle for existence, for every explicitly asserted right implicitly asserts an obligation. Smith's right to a good implies Johnson's obligation to furnish it. One of the principal architects of the rules called rights, Samuel von Pufendorf, noted this property of rights back in 1660, calling rights "ambiguous words."[29] The word "ambiguous" literally means "driving both ways." The first defense against the threat of a right is to point out its ambiguity.

The ability of human beings to determine the rules of the game they play creates a subtle dialectic. How it will all work out we cannot know. But the tragedy of incompatible rights can be averted only by asking the Promethean question *And then what?* People who hate competition, or who are terrified by a Promethean inquiry into the consequences of competition, can play no role in the diminution of tragedy.

Chapter IV

Triage

"Hard cases make bad law," said Justice Holmes.[1] Perhaps so; but they make good science and, I submit, good ethics. What is considered a hard case in ethics is usually one that pits a Promethean approach (which we resist) against an Epimethean (which we slip into all too gratefully). Nowhere is this more apparent than in the problem of allocating scarce resources. One way to do this is by the system called "triage." If there are not enough medical officers to save all the wounded soldiers, whom shall we save *first*? If we don't have enough food to save all the starving people of the world, to whom shall we give the food *first*? Triage gives answers to problems like these.

No full treatment of triage has yet been written. The recently published four-volume *Encyclopedia of Bioethics*[2] treats the subject in a superficial and desultory fashion. For reasons that should become clear as we go along, there is great reluctance to discuss this topic. It may be that the popular media will steal a march on the scholars. For a number of years the Korean War television show, M*A*S*H, has introduced the term "triage" into the dialogue about once every two months (by my estimate). The word is usually just thrown out in passing; it no doubt escapes the notice of most viewers because they are not familiar with it. But in January of 1979 the producers used about five minutes of the program to explain the procedure of medical triage in a dramatically justified context. Their treatment might be criticized for not sufficiently emphasizing the controversial aspects of the system, but it was a good introduction to the subject.

The formerly rare word "triage" was introduced to the general public by the Paddock brothers in 1967, thus starting an argument that is still with us. In their book *Famine—1975!* William Paddock, an agricultural expert specializing in tropical problems, and

Paul Paddock, a retired officer of the U.S. Department of State, defended a simple thesis: America cannot possibly save everyone in the world from starving, so we will have to make choices, following the method of selection known to the military as triage.[3] What is triage?

"Triage," said Lord Ritchie-Calder some time later, "is a relentless two-syllable word. It is a French term dredged up from the mud of the First World War, of the Marne, the Somme, Verdun, Passchendaele and Chateau-Thierry."[4] If we hope to make progress in dealing with so vital an issue we had better refrain from using such emotional language. Let us be advised by Spinoza.

Non ridere, non lugere, neque detestari, sed intelligiere.[5]

"Not to laugh, not to lament, neither to curse, but to understand" —this should be our policy and our goal. It should be noted that Lord Ritchie-Calder gained his reputation and his peerage from his work as a journalist: the significance of this vocation will be touched on later.

Before evaluating the Paddocks' proposal to apply triage in the distribution of food let us see how the practice is carried out in a strictly military situation, relying on the excellent discussion by Stuart W. Hinds in a symposium on *Lifeboat Ethics*.[6] Military triage is a system of assigning priority for the treatment of the wounded after a battle WHENEVER *the need for medical attention exceeds the supply of medical personnel and facilities.* (The italicized phrase is important but often overlooked.) In such cases the wounded can be categorized into three groups:

Group One: Those so seriously wounded that they either cannot survive, or can be saved only if served by an unreasonably large allotment of medical resources.

Group Two: Those who can be saved by a reasonable amount of care, but would die without it.

Group Three: Those who will survive without treatment (though possibly with some pain)—the so-called "walking wounded." In any event, their treatment can be postponed to a later time when the activity is less hectic.

A system of military triage was described and first consciously used by Baron Dominque Jean Larrey (1766–1842), Napoleon's surgeon-in-chief. I say "consciously used" because I suspect that such a judgmental scheme has often been employed in times of scarcity: triage is common sense. It is worth noting that Baron Larrey also introduced the field ambulance to military medicine, for which hundreds of thousands of soldiers have been thankful.

As with so many human innovations, the *naming* of triage in medicine did not come until long after its rationale was explained. The literature on military triage is not large; the very paucity of it throws light on human motives and the origin of taboos. The word "triage" does not occur in the indexes of either *Military Medicine* (twenty-five volumes) or *Military Surgeon* (ninety-three volumes), the two journals devoted exclusively to military medicine. The word does not appear in any articles dealing with war casualties, the evacuation of casualties, first aid, or the treatment of battle casualties. Instead, we find the words "sorting," "selection," "selective tagging," and the like.

"Triage" is not found in the index of any of the fourteen volumes of the British *History of the Second World War*, but it does occur a score of times in the American equivalent. (Why the national difference?) On one occasion a British military surgeon remarked:

> The word "triage" has been quite rightfully condemned. I think it is outlived, and some more sensible word such as grouping, or selection is the word of choice. I don't think it matters very much that we have three groups a, b and c; or one, two and three. That, after all, is intended only as a guide for one who hasn't faced it before. It is . . . sense that matters.

Plainly the commentator is disturbed only by the word, not the fact. "Words," said Thomas Hobbes, "are wise men's counters,— they do but reckon by them; but they are the money of fools." How, then, is a wise man to counsel with fools? If the counterfeit is accepted as genuine, ideas will be lost through confusion; but if the counterfeit is publicly identified for what it is, passions may be so aroused that ideas are rejected without examination.

Part of the emotional reaction to triage stems, I think, from a mistaken assumption as to the etymology of the word. "Triage"

looks like it comes from "tri-" or three, and this suggests a necessary division into three groups, with the subsequent absolute rejection of one group, the "hopelessly wounded." Absolute rejection frightens us: to reword an old saw, we fear that the life
that is rejected may be our own.

But "triage" has quite a different origin: it comes from the
French *trier* which means to sort, sort out, screen, pick, choose,
cull, select. When someone speaks against triage but in favor of
sorting or selection he is guilty of etymological nonsense. Sorting
is sorting, whatever the word used, and the word "triage" was
used for the sorting of wools and coffee beans long before it was
applied to the sorting of human casualties.

The three-way sorting scheme is a good pedagogical tool for
explaining the logic of triage, but trifurcation is not necessary.
Alternatively we can arrange the candidates for help into a single
hierarchical list based on efficiency, where efficiency is measured
by the "amount of life" (L) saved per unit effort (E), as expressed
in the L/E ratio. The individuals we earlier spoke of as Group
Two will be at the head of the list, because their L/E values are
high. Below them will be the other two groups: Group One—the
desperately wounded—have a low L/E value because E is so great;
Group Three—the "walking wounded"—have a low L/E value
because L is so small. (It is understood, of course, that L stands not
for life itself, but for "life saved"—the life that would, without intervention, be lost.) Using an efficiency analysis the pedagogical
trifurcation disappears.

Triage is, then, the most efficient procedure, the procedure that
saves the maximum number of lives. Some sensitive people may
react adversely to the *word* "efficient" applied to the saving of
human lives, but I think it unlikely that such people will reject the
ideal of saving the maximum number of lives possible. Though
the military strategist may want to do this for strictly military
reasons, the most compassionate pacifist reaches the same conclusion by another route. Triage is also the philosophy of choice in
civilian medicine whenever need overwhelms medical resources,
as it may following a massive catastrophe. *No close student of the
problems of either military medicine or civilian medicine has ever
proposed an alternative to triage.*

We are now ready to turn to the application of triage in allocating the "surplus" food of a rich country to poor countries in
need. The book *Famine—1975!* was a shocker to reviewers. The
book reviewer of the *Christian Science Monitor*[7] was repelled
by its "self-righteousness," pointing to its subtitle, "America's
Decision: Who Will Survive?" The facts behind this title are
simple: America exports about half of the cereal grains it produces, and more than half of the grain in international trade is
produced by the United States. If we sell grain, its distribution
is determined by market mechanisms; but when we give it away,
if there are more requests than we can fulfill, how can we avoid
deciding who gets how much? In years when demand exceeds
supply we must triage the distribution—yes, triage is now an
English verb—and the most hopeless countries would have to do
without. The internationalist Richard Falk has objected to *our*
making such decisions:

> Such an approach involves a radical repudiation of human soli-
> darity, requires standing aside while millions perish, and natu-
> rally induces the society called "hopeless" to adopt the most des-
> perate strategies of self-preservation. As such, *triage* is danger-
> ously naive about political consequences.[8]

Without undue simplification I think the issues raised by Falk
can be fairly dealt with in a few words. First let us take up the
matter of political naivety. If we are thinking of war we must remember that modern warfare is so expensive that even the richest
nations cannot afford it: the "Yom Kippur War" in 1973, waged
in proxy for the Soviet Union and the United States, though it
lasted only eighteen days, nearly bankrupted us. For poor countries, *invasive* foreign wars are out of the question. As for terrorism, the threat of it will be with us as long as envy exists—
that is, forever—so we have to find ways to deal with it anyway.
The threat of terrorism, like other forms of blackmail, cannot be
bought off; police action, imperfect though it be, is the principal
recourse of a society that is determined to survive.

Falk says that resorting to triage "requires standing aside while
millions perish." But if a 100 million ton supply of surplus grain
encounters a 200 million ton demand, what more can we do than

"stand aside"? Further activity would, at best, be a waste of resources; and at worst, counter-productive. The implication of "standing aside" is that we do so callously. Critics of triage sometimes sound as though their principal concern is that the rich should suffer. (The critics assume the role of deputies of envy.) But what is the good of emotional suffering? *Com-passion* literally means "sympathy with." Does compassion that leads to no useful action do the unfortunate any good? Triage may be enriched with compassion, or it may not be. If you had to choose between people practicing the two kinds of triage, which would you choose? If you had to be operated on, what would you look for first in your surgeon—competence or compassion?

There are those who reject triage on the grounds that it is not necessary. Of course if it isn't, if there is no real scarcity, then there is no need to triage the applicants. But the denial of scarcity is generally made *sotto voce*. When Falk discusses the group to be left out of the distribution of goods in international triage he uses quotation marks to surround the word "hopeless" thus impugning the idea of scarcity.

The reviewer in the *Monitor* denied the grounds for triage in a different way: "Since we cannot condemn India—or Haiti or Egypt—to death, since countries and people cannot simply vanish from the face of the earth, what heroic answer must be found?" What a multi-edged sword language is! "Condemn" suggests sentencing under criminal law, but the reason for the discrimination of triage is not to condemn but to maximize the number of lives saved. "Condemn" is an Epimethean judgment that takes no account of the successful Promethean strategy of triage. As for any countries and people vanishing from the face of the earth, nations—a non-living abstraction—have vanished before, and they will continue to vanish. *Individual* people may die "before their time," but the abstraction called *the people* is almost ineradicable. Twenty-five percent of the European populace was extinguished by plague in the middle of the fourteenth century, but "the people" continued and are now more numerous than ever.

Those who cannot bring themselves to admit the Promethean rationality of triage are inclined to befuddle the issue by professing a pretty faith in counterfactual conditionals. The *Monitor* reviewer's "what heroic answer must be found?" implies that there *is* a "heroic" and painlessly acceptable answer. Aurelio Peccei, a rich industrialist turned internationalist,[9] speaking of the making of triage decisions, asserts that "the right to make such decisions cannot be left to just a few nations, because it would lend them ominous power over the life of the world's hungry. However, the world has yet to see any international mechanism to cope with these human, moral and political dilemmas."[10] In other words, triage decisions must be turned over to a supranational authority—which does not exist! And if no one is empowered to carry out triage, more lives will be lost.

There is an old folk saying that should be worked into a sampler to hang in the study of every idealist: *"If if's and and's were pots and pans, there'd be no need for tinkers."*

People who refuse to face squarely the challenge of scarcity are apt to find themselves in embarrassing positions. I cite two instances, the first from a newspaper account:

> An Irish nun is visiting Bangladesh, staying at a Christian hostel in Dacca. On her second evening in the city, she steps outside for a breath of air and finds an emaciated baby deserted on the doorstep. She takes the baby in, feeds it, doctors it, bathes it, and then goes out searching for the mother, who is nowhere to be found.
>
> The next morning the nun finds a second starving baby lying in the street in front of the hostel. So she takes the second baby in. Then she goes off to the local police station to report the missing babies and to seek advice.
>
> The advice is to put the babies back in the street or, the police officer says, you will find four more babies tomorrow.
>
> "What on earth am I to do?" the nun says later in the day. "Am I to put them out to starve?"[11]

Note that the moral is left dangling. Whether or not the nun finally saw the light, it is contrary to the traditions of journalism to reach a conclusion in such an emotionally threatening situation. We are lucky when a newspaper even clearly points out the problem.

The second account is of Mother Teresa, the European nun who has devoted a lifetime to bringing comfort to the poor of Calcutta. It is commonly estimated that a quarter of a million of India's poorest people sleep on the streets of Calcutta. Many of them die every night, and are removed by municipal drays. Many others, near death, have trouble moving the next morning. Some of these are picked up by Mother Teresa's workers and carried away to her rest home where they are bathed, put in clean apparel, and fed. The idea is to give them a dignified death. One cannot but admire the selfless service of these nuns, carrying out duties that would appall most of us. Yet there is irony in the consequences.

Normally the Indian who is so treated dies within a few days; he was selected for this treatment because he appeared to be a terminal case. But judgment is difficult, and some of the rescued survive. What then? The bed of a survivor is needed for a new candidate for death (for Calcutta's nocturnal sidewalks and alcoves furnish a more than bountiful supply). So the recovered Indian is put out on the sidewalks—"to try again," as it were. Sooner or later he will fulfill the implied contract. In the meantime Mother Teresa, rejecting conventional triage, is forced to practice a sort of triage of her own. Proponents of traditional triage see an ironical justice in this punishment. We cannot refrain from asking, Does Mother Teresa increase or decrease the amount of suffering in the world?

Unwillingness to make hard decisions extends to other species. When the *Torrey Canyon* oil-tanker wrecked off British shores, the spilled oil covered the feathers of thousands of birds. British volunteers, great bird-lovers, flocked to save the birds by cleaning the oil off their feathers. Experts, assessing the results later, found that most of the birds perished before they were cleaned, and that most of the few that survived the cleaning process died when they were released. One of the directors of the project told the London *Sunday Times*: "These bird-rescue centres have been established because we haven't the guts to say there is nothing we can do. It is only a public-relations exercise."[12]

Public relations is a great breeder of hypocrisy. The *appearance* of compassion pays—as every actor, preacher, politician, and public relations specialist knows very well, though it is to his hypocritical interest not to dwell on the fact. The profession of journalism also selects for the appearance of compassion (accompanied, we can grant, by some genuine feeling).

Of every well-intentioned proposal we must ask the Promethean question *And then what?* for time is of the essence. An act is generally identified as compassionate if it diminishes suffering *right now*: we seldom demand of a compassionate act that it diminish suffering a decade from now. Those who pride themselves on compassionately rejecting triage do so because they hold it unthinkable to ask people to suffer in the present for the sake of a brighter future for others or for themselves.

Journalism, by its nature, is oriented almost wholly toward the present, a very narrow present indeed for daily newspapers. It is perfectly natural that journalists should be strong on present-oriented compassion and weak on Promethean concern for the future consequences of present action. Journalist Lord Ritchie-Calder's abhorrence of the word "triage" is easily understandable in terms of his occupation, as is also his opinion that M*A*S*H is a heartless and inhumane television program.[13] He is much disturbed by the joking that goes on among the doctors during the hectic operating scenes. Mankind's never-ending struggle against hypocrisy would be helped if Lord Ritchie-Calder would listen to Lord Byron:

> *And if I laugh at any mortal thing,*
> *'Tis that I may not weep.*[14]

There is much unpreventable tragedy in the world, and bitter laughter comes naturally to those whose vocation requires prolonged attendance at scenes of tragedy. Taking a cue from Sir Toby Belch who asked, "Dost thou think, because thou art virtuous, there shall be no more cakes and ale?"[15] we might well ask, *"Because thou art compassionate, shall there be no more gales of laughter?"* There are times when laughter is desperately needed to enable us to retain our sanity in this tragic world. But it must be admitted that the cause of our laughter can be easily misunderstood by compassionate men and women who have not squarely faced the implications of scarcity.

As the Promethean approach to ethics gains in acceptance we will become ever more aware of tragedy and the necessity of weighing the good of present actions against their contingent future consequences. The vocational ethics of the physician—as presently conceived—require that he focus only on the present person. Who, then, speaks for posterity? This Promethean problem has been poignantly stated by the English physiologist A. V. Hill:

> The dilemma is this. All the impulses of decent humanity, all the dictates of religion and all the traditions of medicine insist that suffering should be relieved, curable diseases cured, preventable disease prevented. The obligation is regarded as unconditional: it is not permitted to argue that the suffering is due to folly, that the children are not wanted, that the patient's family would be happier if he died. All that may be so; but to accept it as a guide to action would lead to a degradation of standards of humanity by which civilization would be permanently and indefinitely poorer. . . .
>
> Some might [take] the purely biological view that if men will breed like rabbits they must be allowed to die like rabbits. . . . Most people would still say no. But suppose it were certain now that the pressure of increasing population, uncontrolled by disease, would lead not only to widespread exhaustion of the soil and of other capital resources but also to continuing and increasing international tension and disorder, making it hard for civilization itself to survive: Would the majority of humane and reasonable people then change their minds? If ethical principles deny our right to do evil in order that good may come, are we justified in doing good when the foreseeable consequence is evil?[16]

The compassionate Promethean is not satisfied by the mere saving of a present life: he wants us to find some way of taking account of the future and of posterity's needs.[17] The Promethean cannot forget that the life we save today breeds more lives in need of saving tomorrow.

This insight is not new. Tertullian, in the third century, spoke of "the vast population of the earth to which we are a burden," saying that "she scarcely can provide for our needs." In modern terms, all population theory must begin with the concept of the carrying capacity of the territory (the earth, for example).[18] "Our demands grow greater," said Tertullian. Does it occur to us to moderate our demands by bringing supply and demand into balance? No, not even in Tertullian's day: "Our complaints against nature's inadequacy are heard by all." In other words, don't blame ourselves, blame someone else (Nature). If that is the best we can do, we recognize a bitter justification for Tertullian's conclusion:

> The scourges of pestilence, famine, wars, and earthquakes have come to be regarded as a blessing to overcrowded nations, since they serve to prune away the luxuriant growth of the human race.[19]

The concept of carrying capacity is one which any agriculturist understands—notice the verb "to prune" in Tertullian's statement. This understanding was pretty well lost during the hundred and fifty years after Malthus, a time that saw the rise of the idea of progress, an increase in urbanization, and the flowering of urbanized economics, which is the economics of the man who buys his food at the store. Urbanized economics says that the supply of anything can always be increased by raising the price. Urban economists have lost sight of the substantive source of food—the land. Of course technology has tremendously increased the carrying capacity of the land, but it cannot do so indefinitely. And technology is powerless to increase the supply of some goods, for instance wild beauty and natural solitude.

Economists are only now coming to recognize that today's economic interpretation of "scarcity" and "supply" is unecological. Kicking and screaming every inch of the way economists are being dragged into the twenty-first century.[20] They must recapture the vision (blotted out after John Stuart Mill) that economics is above all else the science of the allocation of scarce resources.

To prune, to thin, to cull, to sort out, to screen, to pick, to choose, to select—every one of these actions takes time into account. We renounce some present good for the sake of the future. To the critic who is deficient in a feeling for the future, selection processes bespeak a lack of compassion. But those who have the courage to select, and to live with the consequences of selection, believe that only Promethean, time-oriented decisions deserve the name of compassion.

Every system of ethics (like all logical systems) rests on unexamined assumptions. Throughout this discussion I have assumed that it is desirable to minimize suffering. When it comes to the saving of lives most people, given the choice of saving many lives or few, would choose many. The theory of triage seeks to maximize the number of lives saved. The philosopher John Taurek[21] has argued that triage is not the best policy. Taurek's hints of the mathematical form of his argument are here developed explicitly.

Nowhere in his discussion does Taurek use the word "triage." Whether this is through ignorance or semantic distaste does not matter: he is clearly talking about triage, which he contrasts with another system. In comparing these two systems I use the terms "Triage Policy" and "Parity Policy." The reason for the second name will presently be explained.

Suppose that we have 5 units of a life-saving medicine; that there are 5 persons in Group I, each of whom requires 1 unit to save his life; and that Group II has only 1 person in it, and that he requires 5 units of the medicine to save his life. Using this model, let us compare the two policies.

Triage Policy: Seeking to maximize the saving of lives we allocate all 5 units of medicine to Group I, thus saving 5 lives. The single person in Group II gets no medicine. Triage Policy saves 5 of the 6 lives at risk. Triage specifically recognizes the inequality of individuals, the significant inequality in this connection being the inequality of demands on environmental resources. (The resources are environmental because they are not internal to the individual making the demands.) If the relevant sector of the environment is controlled by the community, the right of allocation may be reserved to the community, acting through its legitimated authorities.

Parity Policy: Taurek maintains that policy should be built on equal concern for each person, regardless of the inequality of the demands (needs). (Here we hear an echo of Marx's "to each according to his needs.") I think it is fair to call Taurek's proposal a Parity Policy. Such a policy seeks to give each petitioner an equal chance at life, no matter how large his demands on the resources of the environment. To do this Taurek proposes that we begin by flipping a coin to see whether the 5 units of medicine are to be assigned wholly to Group I or wholly to Group II. In that way, everyone is given a 50-50 chance of being saved. No one is penalized because his need is greater.

How many lives are saved under this policy? We must bring probability theory into play, employing the concept of "mathematical expectation" (M.E.).

Fifty percent of the time 5 lives are saved. This gives a partial M.E. of $(1/2) (5) = 2 1/2$.

Fifty percent of the time 1 life is saved. Partial M.E. $= (1/2) (1) = 1/2$.

The sum of the above two answers is the total M.E. Total M.E. $= (2 1/2) + (1/2) = 3$.

So the Parity Policy saves—on the average, over the long run—just 3 lives instead of 5.

The efficiency of the Triage Policy, relative to the Parity Policy, is: $5 \div 3 = 1.67$, or 67 percent more efficient in saving lives.

One might suppose that the superiority of the Triage Policy in the saving of human lives would make the philosopher doubt the propriety of his Parity Policy, but he goes out of his way to let us know that he has no doubts. He would pursue it, he says, even if the number 5 were replaced by the number 50 (with the necessary changes). Let us follow him up this path.

We have 50 units of life-saving medicine.

Each of the 50 persons in Group I requires 1 unit to have his life saved.

The single person in Group II requires 50 units.

Triage Policy: All 50 units are supplied to Group I, thus saving 50 lives.

Parity Policy: Each group gets all the medicine 50 percent of the time. On the average, the number of lives saved is (½) (50) + (½) (1) = 25 + ½ = 25½.

The relative efficiency of the Triage Policy is now: 50 ÷ 25½ = 1.96, or 96 percent more efficient.

Now let us carry this argument to the limit. Let: n = the number of persons in Group I; and n=the number of units of medicine available, where: (a) each person in Group I requires 1 unit; and (b) the single person in Group II requires n units.

Following the same line of reasoning as before we find that the relative superiority (in saving lives) of the Triage Policy is given by the expression:

$$n \div \frac{n}{2} + \frac{1}{2}.$$

As the variable n becomes indefinitely large, the constant (½) becomes relatively less and less important. In the limit, as $n \to \infty$, the relative efficiency of Triage Policy becomes:

$$n \div \frac{n}{2} = \frac{2n}{n} = 2,$$

i.e., the Triage Policy, in the limit, is 100 percent better than the Parity Policy.

One of the clearest trends of the past two centuries has been the steady increase in the value placed on the individual human life, independent of its social status or social worth. Laws governing the liability of employers and public officials, medical malpractice judgments, attitudes toward national military service—in these and many other areas there has been a steady growth in the presumption that the individual human life is infinitely precious. Considering that the number of human lives has now swelled to nearly five billion; considering that world population is increasing faster than it ever has before (by about 90 million per year); considering that the earth still has only the 5.983×10^{21} metric tons of matter that it started with when life began about three billion years ago—considering all these facts, as we approach closer and closer the limit of the earth's ability to support the all too abundant human lives, it is rather ironical that we should become more and more concerned about the preservation and well-being of each and every individual human life. Our concern does the heart credit; but I doubt if the mythical Man-from-Mars would have predicted this paradoxical coincidence of historical trends. If the Man-from-Mars is anything of an economic determinist he might well question whether the coincidence will long continue.

How are we to view Taurek's Parity Policy in the light of historical trends? On the one hand it seems to represent a reversal, inasmuch as it assigns more value to the *feelings* of the people being judged than it does to their lives. Parity Policy seeks to maximize concern for feelings, whereas Triage Policy maximizes the number of human lives saved. (Should those who strive for population control lobby for Parity Policy? An interesting suggestion!)

On the other hand, if we ask, "What is the relation of policy to the *individual* human life?" emphasizing "individual" rather than "life," we realize that Taurek's proposal is in the mainstream of increasing individualism in the Western world. As an individual I may want to live forever, to be freed of competitive pressures, and to have my needs taken care of no matter how great the drain on community resources, no matter how many other lives must be sacrificed that I may live. Accused of egotism by others I could conceivably back down on my personal demands. Instead (if I am a thoroughgoing Western-style individualist), I am more likely to take the other tack and recommend that we all support each other in unmitigated individualistic demands, even when the universalizing of these demands proves counter-productive. The replacement of a Triage Policy by a Parity Policy reduces the number of lives saved, or (in less extreme situations) the average quality of people's lives. The true Promethean, concerned with a distant future in which he may no longer be an actor, inevitably is less concerned with individuals *as such* (including himself), and more concerned with the good that accrues to individuals through their membership in a community. In an increasingly more crowded community, in a world pressing ever harder against physical and psychological limits, a true Promethean cannot but support the rationalism of triage policies which, by their very nature, acknowledge the limitedness of the available resources and the limitlessness of time.

At the beginning of this chapter I said that hard cases make good ethics. The scarcity case is a good example. Exploring the implications of the Parity Policy we have discovered that the wisdom of triage can be fully appreciated only if we recognize the inevitability of competition; and competition between members of the same species is inescapable so long as death is not a sufficiently effective thinning agent—which we prevent it from being with our fantastic medical advances. Life, cooperation, and compassion are all good things, but we can have too much of any one good thing, considered in isolation and elevated to the status of an absolute good. The central problem—both philosophically and practically—is to find acceptable ways of weighing opposing goods (under a variety of circumstances and with due regard for the interests of our posterity) so that we—and our descendants—can lead healthy and balanced lives. In this search, Prometheus should be our guide.

Notes

Chapter 1: The Promethean Approach

1. "Technological progress" is the current version of the idea of progress, the history of which is told in J. B. Bury, 1932. *The Idea of Progress* (New York: St. Martin's Press; reprint ed., New York: Dover, 1955). Further documentation is to be found in the valuable collection of readings edited by Frederick J. Teggart, 1949. *The Idea of Progress* (Berkeley: University of California Press).

Though conceived in ancient times the idea was not fully born until the posthumous publication, in 1795, of Condorcet's work (reprinted in 1955 by The Noonday Press of New York). The title Condorcet selected is significant: *Sketch for a Historical Picture of the Progress of the Human Mind*. As I try to make clear in the text, the variant called "technological progress" is largely a mindless progress—and therein lies the trouble. (We must not blame Condorcet for too much.)

2. Garrett Hardin, 1972. *Exploring New Ethics for Survival: The Voyage of the Spaceship Beagle* (New York: Viking), p. 141. Reprinted in 1973 by Penguin Books.

3. Freeman J. Dyson, 1974. "The Hidden Costs of Saying No!" *Bulletin of the Atomic Scientists* 31 (6):23–27.

4. H. J. Rose, 1959. *A Handbook of Greek Mythology* (New York: Dutton).

5. Hardin, *Exploring New Ethics for Survival*, chapter 7.

6. Miguel de Cervantes Saavedra, 1605. *Don Quixote de la Mancha*, book 1, chapter 6.

7. John Sparrow, 1977. *Too Much of a Good Thing* (Chicago: University of Chicago Press).

8. Ernest Partridge, 1979. Personal communication.

9. Martin Buber, 1937. *I and Thou* (New York: Scribner's, 1970).

10. Garrett Hardin, 1974. "The Rational Foundation of Conservation," *North American Review* 259 (4):14–17.

11. Joseph Fletcher, 1966. *Situation Ethics* (Philadelphia: Westminster Press).

12. In seeking a suitable name for this approach I have discarded the alternative possibilities of *bioethics* and *ecological ethics*, the former because it is already too firmly identified with some rather narrow problems encountered in medical practice (about which too much nonsense has been written), and the latter because it suggests a restriction to such environmental problems as pollution. "Promethean ethics" can encompass all the problems of these two named disciplines, and more; it emphasizes the approach, rather than the material on which it works.

Chapter II: Death

1. Jessica Mitford, 1963. *The American Way of Death* (New York: Simon & Schuster).

2. John Milton, 1667. *Paradise Lost*, book 1, line 22.

3. Richard D. Alexander, 1967. "The Evolution of Genitalia and Mating Behavior in Crickets (Gryllidae) and Other Orthoptera," *Miscellaneous Publications of the Museum of Zoology, University of Michigan* 133:1–62.

4. For an understanding of sociobiology see any of the following books.

Monograph: Edward O. Wilson, 1975. *Sociobiology: The New Synthesis* (Cambridge: Harvard University Press).

Textbook: David P. Barash, 1977. *Sociobiology and Behavior* (New York: Elsevier).

Popularization: Richard Dawkins, 1976. *The Selfish Gene* (New York: Oxford University Press).

5. J. Koskimies, 1950. "The Life of the Swift, *Micropus apus* (L.), in Relation to the Weather," *Annales Academiae Scientarum*

Fennicea, Series A, IV. Biologica 12:1–151. Reprinted in David E. Davis, ed., 1974. *Behavior as an Ecological Factor* (Stroudsburg, Pa.: Dowden, Hutchinson & Ross; distributed by John Wiley & Sons).

6. R. A. Fisher, 1930. *The Genetical Theory of Natural Selection* (reprint ed., New York: Dover, 1958).

7. P. B. Medawar, 1957. *The Uniqueness of the Individual* (London: Methuen).

8. Garrett Hardin, 1963. "The Impact of Longevity on Society, and Vice Versa," *Proceedings of the Third National Conference of the Joint Council to Improve the Health of the Aged* (Chicago: Joint Council to Improve Health Care of the Aged).

9. Garrett Hardin, 1977. *The Limits of Altruism* (Bloomington: Indiana University Press). See also: Garrett Hardin and John Baden, eds., 1977. *Managing the Commons* (San Francisco: W. H. Freeman).

10. Garrett Hardin, 1978. *Stalking the Wild Taboo* (2nd ed., Los Altos, Calif.: Kaufmann), p. 172. The chapter is a reprint of an article first published in 1963. The sense of the aphorism is surely millennia old, but since it threatens the dreams of naive Epimethean reformers it must, apparently, constantly be rediscovered and clothed in new language.

11. Garrett Hardin, 1968. "The Tragedy of the Commons," *Science* 162:1243–48. (Also reprinted in Hardin and Baden, eds., *Managing the Commons*.) What one might call "the necessary solitude of a maximum" speedily impresses itself on anyone who studies partial differentiation, and must have been known at least as far back as D'Alembert (1717–83), though the truth is seldom developed explicitly. This is another of the ideas that threaten the dreams of naive Epimetheans.

12. *Ecclesiastes* 3:1–3.

13. I first advanced the blueprint image in 1967. See chapters 2 and 3 in Hardin, *Stalking the Wild Taboo.*

14. Garrett Hardin, 1974. *Mandatory Motherhood: The True Meaning of "Right to Life"* (Boston: Beacon Press).

15. Norman E. Himes, 1936. *Medical History of Contraception* (reprint ed., New York: Gamut Press, 1963).

16. George Devereaux, 1955. *A Study of Abortion in Primitive Societies* (New York: Julian Press).

17. Garrett Hardin, 1969. *Population, Evolution and Birth Control* (2nd ed., San Francisco: W. H. Freeman), p. 281. (Also reprinted on page 46 of Hardin, *Stalking the Wild Taboo*.)

18. James C. Mohr, 1978. *Abortion in America* (New York: Oxford University Press).

19. Mary Steichen Calderone, ed., 1958. *Abortion in the United States* (New York: Hoeber-Harper).

20. F. A. von Hayek, 1978. "The Three Sources of Human Values." (Separatum, p. 8.) Scheduled for republication in 1979 in volume 3 of the author's *Law, Legislation and Liberty* (Chicago: University of Chicago Press).

21. Raymond S. Duff and A. G. M. Campbell, 1973. "Moral and Ethical Dilemmas in the Special-Care Nursery." *New England Journal of Medicine* 289:890–94.

22. Marvin Kohl, ed., 1978. *Infanticide and the Value of Life* (Buffalo: Prometheus Books).

23. J. D. Bernal, 1967. "The Struggle with Death," *New Scientist*, 12 January, p. 87.

24. Jonathan Swift, 1726. *Travels into Several Remote Nations of the World by Lemuel Gulliver*, third voyage, chapter 10.

25. Theodore B. Schwartz, 1978. "The Spectre of Decrepitude," *New England Journal of Medicine* 299:1248–49.

26. Miguel de Unamuno, 1912. *The Tragic Sense of Life* (reprint ed., New York: Dover, 1954), p. 40.

27. I use the word "operational" in the sense established, and nearly universally accepted in science, by the physicist Percy W. Bridgman. See his *The Logic of Modern Physics* (New York: Macmillan, 1927) and *The Intelligent Individual and Society* (New York: Macmillan, 1938). On page 90 of the latter he says: "I have never come across a term of mystical or supernatural import which did not, as a matter of fact, eventually dissolve on analysis into something whose meaning was to be found only in the operations of substituting it into some verbal form. Particularly in philosophy and religion have our verbalisms run away with us like wildfire. The whole structure is so permeated by this intel-

lectual cancer that my own instinct is just to scrap all traditional philosophy and religion and start again from the beginning."

28. Samuel G. F. Brandon, 1974. "Death Rites and Customs," *Encyclopaedia Britannica* 5:533.

29. Epicurus. *Letter to Meneoceus.*

30. Joseph Fletcher, 1967. *Moral Responsibility* (Philadelphia: Westminster Press), p. 144.

31. Logan Pearsall Smith, 1931. *Afterthoughts.*

32. Hallam Tennyson, 1974. "Interview," *The Listener*, 29 August, p. 275.

33. George Moore, 1886. *Confessions of a Young Man* (New York: Brentano's, 1920), pp. 8–9.

34. *Life*, 21 August 1964, p. 33.

35. Herman Feifel, 1963. "Death," in Norman L. Farberow, ed., *Taboo Topics* (New York: Atherton Press).

36. Ivan Illich et al., 1977. *Disabling Professions* (London: Marion Boyars).

37. C. William Hall, Domingo Liotta, and Michael E. De-Bakey, 1967. "Artificial Heart—Present and Future," in *Research in the Service of Man* (Washington: U.S. Government Printing Office), pp. 201–2.

38. Hugh Morrison, 1955. "Letter to the Editor," *Time*, 21 November, pp. 6, 8.

39. Elisabeth Kübler-Ross, 1969. *On Death and Dying* (London: Macmillan).

40. Keyfitz's estimate is to be found in Annabelle Desmond, 1962. "How Many People Have Ever Lived on Earth?" *Population Bulletin* 18, no. 1. The figure given is 77 billion; I have updated it to the year 1980.

Chapter III: Competition

1. Garrett Hardin, 1978. *Stalking the Wild Taboo* (2nd ed., Los Altos, Calif.: Kaufmann), pp. 143–47.

2. Peter L. Berger and Brigitte Berger, 1972. *Sociology* (New York: Basic Books), p. 173.

3. The *Origin of Species* was published in 1859. The quotations given here are from the last, the sixth, edition (1872), of which there are many printings. My citations are to a printing by Macmillan of New York, in 1927. For each citation I give both chapter and page number. The presently cited passage occurs in chapter 3, on page 59.

4. *In Memoriam.* This poem was begun shortly after the death of the poet's friend Arthur Hallam, in 1833, but was not published until 1849.

5. *Origin,* chapter 3, p. 59.

6. *Origin,* chapter 3, p. 73.

7. *Origin,* chapter 15, p. 525. As usual, I have used the words of the sixth edition. The first edition does not have the words "by the Creator" in the last sentence. Darwin, an agnostic at this time and to the end of his life, added the words in response to social pressure, probably mostly that of his beloved wife. He was at times somewhat ashamed for having yielded.

8. Loren Eiseley, 1959. "Charles Darwin, Edward Blyth, and the Theory of Natural Selection," *Proceedings of the American Philosophical Society* 103:94–108. Eiseley shows that Darwin knew of Blyth's work which he incorporated into his own, largely without credit. Such behavior is very unlike Darwin, who usually leaned over backwards to give others credit. The explanation is probably this: he read Blyth's papers *before* October 1838 when, as he says, "I happened to read for amusement Malthus on Population, [as a consequence of which] I had at last got a theory by which to work." The ideas of others that come to us before we have a framework to set them in are all too likely to be absorbed without their authors' names, so to speak, to be reworked at the unconscious level and to be regurgitated later without credit. This is an honest, though lamentable, source of plagiarism.

9. In speaking of heredity in terms of genes rather than codons of nucleic acids I am being somewhat less than up-to-date, but I want to keep the language simple. Rephrasing the arguments in terms of nucleic acids will make the practical conclusions presented here even stronger. See chapter 2 of Curt Stern, 1973. *Principles of Human Genetics* (3rd ed., San Francisco: W. H. Freeman).

10. Eliot Howard, 1920. *Territory in Bird Life* (London: Collins). Portions of this classic are reprinted in Allen W. Stokes, ed., 1974. *Territory* (Stroudsburg, Pa.: Dowden, Hutchinson & Ross; distributed by John Wiley & Sons).

11. Jonathan K. Waage, 1979. "Dual Function of the Damselfly Penis: Sperm Removal and Transfer," *Science* 203:916–18.

12. Garrett Hardin, 1960. "The Competitive Exclusion Principle," *Science* 131:1292–97. Reprinted in Robert H. Whittaker and Simon A. Levin, eds., 1975. *Niche: Theory and Application* (Stroudsburg, Pa.: Dowden, Hutchinson & Ross; distributed by John Wiley & Sons).

13. Garrett Hardin, 1959. *Nature and Man's Fate* (New York: Rinehart), pp. 83–89.

14. For an explicit presentation of the mathematics see Garrett Hardin, 1963. "The Cybernetics of Competition," *Perspective in Biology and Medicine* 7:58–84. This has been reprinted in Hardin, *Stalking the Wild Taboo*, where the mathematics appears on page 159.

15. Hardin, *Nature and Man's Fate*, pp. 86–87.

16. For reasons developed in the next section on ecological succession, actual *exclusion* is seldom verified in nature. For a documented case see Paul DeBach, Robert M. Hendrickson, Jr., and Mike Rose, 1978. "Competitive Displacement: Extinction of the Yellow Scale, *Aonidiella citrina* (Coq.) (Homoptera: Diaspididae), by its Ecological Homologue, the California Red Scale, *Aonidiella avrantii* (Mask.) in Southern California," *Hilgardia* 46 (1):1–35.

17. Piercy Ravenstone, 1821. *A Few Doubts as to the Correctness of some Opinions generally entertained on the Subjects of Population and Political Economy* (London: John Andrews; facsimile reprint by Augustus M. Kelley, New York, 1966), p. 203. The context of Ravenstone's *obiter dictum* is more economic than political, but there can be little doubt of its generality. Joseph Dorfman, in his introduction to the Kelley reprint, presents evidence that Ravenstone is the pseudonym of a no less obscure Anglican clergyman, Edward Edwards.

18. The meaning of the neologism "pejoristic" should be obvious from the context. For a lengthy discussion see my essay

"Pejorism: the Middle Way" in *Stalking the Wild Taboo.*

19. Benjamin Nelson, 1969. *The Idea of Usury: From Tribal Brotherhood to Universal Otherhood* (2nd ed., Chicago: University of Chicago Press).

20. John Maynard Keynes, 1931. *Essays in Persuasion* (reprint ed., New York: Norton, 1963). See the last essay, "Economic Possibilities for our Grandchildren," first published in 1930.

21. Taken from the January 1979 issue of *Conservation Foundation Letter* (Washington, D.C.), an excellent discussion of the perils of modern information control.

22. The Moslem minority within Israel is growing faster than the Jewish majority, so the *internal* problem is getting worse also.

23. U. Thant, 1968, speaking for thirty signatories of a United Nations document. *International Planned Parenthood News,* no. 168, p. 3.

24. *Time,* 23 December 1974, p. 31.

25. *Wall Street Journal,* 7 March 1979, p. 1.

26. Leo Kuper, 1977. *The Pity of It All: Polarization of Racial and Ethnic Relations* (Minneapolis: University of Minnesota Press).

27. Hannah Vogt, 1964. *The Burden of Guilt* (New York: Oxford University Press). After the Second World War had passed far enough into the background, many of the common people of Germany, understandably wishing to minimize their feelings of guilt, tried to cast doubt on the story of the Jewish genocide by asking, "How could we have killed 6 million Jews when there were less than half a million in prewar Germany?" It appears that only 170,000 of the Jews killed were Germans, the rest coming from other countries, notably Poland with its nearly 3 million Polish Jewish victims.

28. Nora Barlow, 1958. *The Autobiography of Charles Darwin* (London: Collins), p. 120.

29. Samuel von Pufendorf, 1660. *Elementorum Jurisprudentia Universalis Libri Duo.* The statement runs: *Jus est potentia moralis activa, personae competens ad aliquid ab altero necessario habendum: Vocabuli ambiguitas.* (See *Encyclopedia of Bioethics,* p. 625.)

Chapter IV: Triage

1. Oliver Wendell Holmes, Jr., 1904. *Northern Securities Co. v. United States, 193 U.S. 197,400.* "Great cases like hard cases make bad law," is what Holmes actually said, which implies that the second part of the quotation is older than Holmes. A case is great when it threatens the culture. The ability of even the wisest jurists to make a balanced cultural change with a single court judgment is severely limited—this is Hayek's point, chapter 2, ref. 20—and so the judgment made in a great case makes bad law in the sense that it has to be followed by a swarm of other judgments and legislation before any new sort of cultural stability is achieved. Consider, for instance, the still unfinished cascade of consequences of the Supreme Court decision in *Brown v. Board of Education*, 1954.

2. Warren T. Reich, ed., 1978. *Encyclopedia of Bioethics* (New York: Free Press).

3. William and Paul Paddock, 1967. *Famine—1975! America's Decision: Who Will Survive?* (Boston: Little, Brown).

4. From "Triage," a dialogue discussion paper for the Center for the Study of Democratic Institutions, Santa Barbara, California, 4 April 1975.

5. I do not know the original source. This passage serves as the epigraph of Ernest Becker, 1973. *The Denial of Death* (New York: Free Press).

6. George R. Lucas, Jr., and Thomas W. Ogletree, eds., 1976. *Lifeboat Ethics: The Moral Dilemmas of World Hunger* (New York: Harper & Row).

7. Henrietta Buckmaster, *Christian Science Monitor*, 9 November 1967.

8. Richard A. Falk, 1971. *This Endangered Planet* (New York: Random House).

9. Peccei is the founder and *primum inter pares* of the informal "Club of Rome," which catalyzed the production of the *Limits to Growth* study by a group at the Massachusetts Institute of Technology.

10. Aurelio Peccei, 1977. *The Human Quality* (New York: Pergamon Press).

11. *The Wall Street Journal,* 27 November 1974, p. 1.

12. Noël Mostert, 1974. "Supertankers," *The New Yorker,* 20 May, p. 84.

13. I have heard him express this opinion twice at small conferences. Whether this is in print or not I do not know.

14. George Noel Gordon, Lord Byron, 1821. *Don Juan,* canto 4, stanza 4.

15. William Shakespeare, 1600. *Twelfth-Night,* act 2, scene 3, line 124.

16. A. V. Hill, 1952. "The Ethical Dilemma of Science," *Nature* 170:388–93. As a further footnote let me report that at a symposium in which I took part Lord Ritchie-Calder cited this passage of Lord Hill's as a particularly obnoxious one.

17. This is a fantastically subtle and recalcitrant problem. I have scratched the surface of it in chapter 4 of *The Limits of Altruism* (Bloomington: Indiana University Press, 1977).

18. See chapter 3 of *The Limits of Altruism.*

19. Tertullian. *De Anima.*

20. Herman E. Daly, 1978. *Steady-State Economics* (San Francisco: W. H. Freeman). This is an excellent introduction to the new economics.

21. John M. Taurek, 1977. "Should the Numbers Count?" *Philosophy and Public Affairs* 6 (4):293–316. After completing his analysis Taurek discovered that similar conclusions had been reached by G. E. M. Anscombe, 1967. "Who is Wronged?" *Oxford Review,* no. 5.

Dr. Garrett Hardin, ecologist, educator, author, and former professor of biology and human ecology at the University of California at Santa Barbara, was born in Dallas, Texas, in 1915. He received a B.S. degree from the University of Chicago in 1936 and did graduate work in biology at Stanford University, obtaining a Ph.D. degree in 1941. In 1942, he became a researcher for the Carnegie Institution of Washington at the division of plant biology on the Stanford campus. He withdrew from his research in 1946 to join the faculty of a small liberal arts college that is now the University of California at Santa Barbara. From 1963 until his retirement, Dr. Hardin was professor of human ecology there.

Dr. Hardin took early retirement in June 1978 to devote himself wholeheartedly to his writing. Perhaps his best-known work is his essay "The Tragedy of the Commons," which first appeared in December 1968 in *Science*. Among his well-known books are: *Nature and Man's Fate; Stalking the Wild Taboo; Population, Evolution and Birth Control; Exploring New Ethics for Survival: The Voyage of the Spaceship Beagle;* and *The Limits of Altruism.*

Dr. Hardin has given the Nieuwland Lectures at the University of Notre Dame, the Remson Bird Lectures at Occidental College, and the Messenger Lectures at Cornell University. He was a national visiting lecturer for Phi Beta Kappa in 1970–71 and Sigma Xi in 1972–73. In 1975, the University of Puget Sound bestowed upon him the honorary Doctor of Humanities degree.

Dr. Garrett Hardin is a persuasive voice for ecological sanity. In his lucid, penetrating, and often witty prose, he urges man to consider the complex problems created by his failure to invent acceptable negative feedbacks to substitute for the predators that control all populations except the human.